— Father's Day 1993 —

D0113847

THE DAD ZONE

Reports from the Tender,

Bewildering, and Hilarious

World of Fatherhood

MICHAEL BURKETT

SIMON & SCHUSTER

NEW YORK LONDON TORONTO SYDNEY TOKYO SINGAPORE

SIMON & SCHUSTER
Simon & Schuster Building
Rockefeller Center
1230 Avenue of the Americas
New York, New York 10020

SIMON & SCHUSTER and colophon are registered trademarks
of Simon & Schuster Inc.

Designed by Bonni Leon-Berman

Manufactured in the United States of America

1   3   5   7   9   10   8   6   4   2

Library of Congress Cataloging in Publication Data
Burkett, Michael.
The Dad zone: reports from the tender, bewildering,
and hilarious world of fatherhood/Michael Burkett.
p.   cm.
1. Father and child—United States—Humor.
2. Parenting—United States—Humor.   I. Title.
II. Title: Dad zone.
HQ756.B86   1993
306.874'2'0207—dc20   93–2816
                                                              CIP

ISBN 0-671-79890-1

C O N T E N T S

For Deborah, Matthew, Jessica

and two world-class dads:

my mother, Mickie Good,

and my grandmother,

Esther B. Nelson

INTRODUCTION

It happens, occasionally, in the middle of the night. I wake up screaming in fear that someone might one day mistake "The Dad Zone" for some kind of advice column. In a world where Arnold Schwarzenegger can be mistaken for an actor and edible underwear is considered sexy, there's no telling the potential for gross public error.

I've been a dad for a number of years, and I still don't have any answers. Only big, mind-bending questions. Like, "What is that mysterious, semibouyant brown crud your children leave in your glass whenever they take a sip of your iced tea? Where does it come from? How do they get it through the straw? Does it breed?"

This is not to say I'm totally unqualified to write a weekly syndicated newspaper column about parenting. I have lots of qualifications. In addition to being the shamelessly proud coproducer of a son, now eight, and a daughter, three, I have seen many motion pictures on the subject, including the mutant monster baby movies *It's Alive!* and *It Lives Again,* which I admire for their stark documentary realism.

Still, you are forgiven for wondering how I ended up with this job. And you'll be forgiven for continuing to wonder after I explain it to you.

In 1989, I was the movie critic for a weekly newspaper in Phoenix, Arizona, and happened to be in the building when someone said, "Maybe we should run some kind of parenting column," and someone else said, "Does anybody here have kids?" and someone else said, "Burkett."

If John Gotti, Ma Barker, Joan Crawford, the "Texas Cheerleader

Hit-Mom," or Jeffrey Dahmer's folks had been present instead of me, one of them would now be writing a parenting column. If they weren't dead or otherwise occupied.

Back then I thought, Hey! This is great! When my kids are grown, I'll be able to hand them a detailed, week-by-week journal of their childhood! But now I'm taking a tip from Ward Cleaver and never mentioning to anyone in my family what it is, exactly, that I do for a living. Otherwise the time will come when both my kids will band together, corner me in my office, and break my typing finger.

No judge in the world will blame them. Especially if Exhibit A is the column, reprinted herein, which deals with my son's innocent discovery—at the supper table—that some body parts are more fun to fiddle with than others.

It's bad enough when your parents never let you forget all the inevitable and totally natural and horribly embarrassing social errors you committed as a youngster. Just ask my brother. When he was about three, he got up in the middle of the night, sleepwalked into the kitchen, opened the silverware drawer, and relieved himself all over Mom's prized cutlery.

To this day, whenever there's a family get-together of any size, someone will bring up the incident and my brother will mutter, "I was only *three,* fer crying' out loud! I was *asleep!* How many times do I gotta hear that story . . ."

This has been going on for over forty-two years and it's my guess that he's starting to get tired of it.

But my brother has it easy. His one little childhood faux pas never left the family living room (until this moment, anyway. Now HE'LL want to break my typing finger). My kids' misadventures, on the other hand, are conveniently home-delivered to total strangers all over North America.

What worries me is that I am forever meeting readers who can quote lines I wrote years ago, syllable for syllable. Like elephants (exceptionally well-read elephants) they never forget.

Therefore, it's not difficult to imagine my son's first date eight or nine years from now. He'll be invited to the girl's house for dinner. He'll walk in, shake hands with her folks, and introduce himself just like the proper young gentleman we attempted to raise.

"Burkett ... Burkett," the girl's mother will say, scratching her head. "Aren't you the boy who can't keep his hands out of his pants at the supper table?"

That's when my son will come home, corner me in my office, and break *all* my fingers. If my brother hasn't beaten him to it.

Ah, well. If four years of reader mail has taught me anything, it is this: There isn't *anything* about parenthood that isn't 100 percent universal. And chief among our common bonds is the fact that it is virtually impossible for moms and dads to read a book all the way through while their children are begging for attention, trying to kill each other, spray-painting the family cat, or piercing their noses and threatening to have their names legally changed to Chunk E. Spew.

I just so happen to have an answer to that dilemma: The first page of this book is blank and has been cleverly designed to be ripped out, torn in half, and wadded into customized, reusable earplugs.

Don't mention it.

Oh, yes. And if my son ever dates your daughter, don't mention the supper-table business, either.

Jesus Swiped My Goldfish

The morning coffee had yet to complete the perk cycle when my three-year-old son hollered, "Daddy! Come look!"

I get this request about three thousand times a day. There was no reason to suspect I was being summoned to view anything more unusual than a Lego spaceship, a wooden-block spaceship, or a Pop-Tart spaceship. So I ignored him. How was I to know we'd had a death in the family?

"Daddy! Come look! Tibbish is sleeping!"

That's when I realized there was real trouble in the living room. If goldfish do sleep, they don't do it upside-down at the top of the tank. Not even if they're trained Hollywood stunt fish.

We'd purchased Tibbish several days before at Woolworth's. My son liked him because he had a black spot on his back. I liked him because he cost twelve cents. My wife liked him as soon as she was absolved of all care, feeding, and aquarium-cleaning duties.

As we headed home, I asked my son what he'd be naming his new pal. He said, "Tibbish." At least that's what we thought he said. Maybe he was just clearing his throat or spitting up. Whatever the case, Tibbish it was.

If you have never owned goldfish, let me describe the experience to you in painstaking detail: You buy them, you take them home, you put them in water, and they die. Not always right away, but soon, and almost always from underfeeding. All goldfish food boxes bear the bold-print warning "DO NOT OVERFEED!" But they don't say a damn thing about underfeeding.

Also, goldfish only die when they know their teensy bug-eyed corpses will be discovered by a small child.

"See, Daddy? Tibbish is *sleeping.*"

"Yes, son," I replied. "He certainly is. Fish don't get more asleep than that."

Sensing that Tibbish would be napping for a while, my son ran off to destroy something in his room. Seizing the moment, I scooped up Tibbish, strolled ever-so-nonchalantly to the bathroom, held a brief funeral service over the porcelain goldfish depository so conveniently built into every home, and flushed the deceased to fish heaven.

It wasn't until midafternoon that my son discovered Tibbish had apparently roused from his snooze, taken a good look at his humble surroundings, and decided he'd be happier elsewhere.

"Daddy! Tibbish is gone!"

"Uh, yes, son. He had to, um, go away."

"Where's Tibbish?"

Now, I probably could have said Elko, Nevada, and that would have been the end of that. Instead I chose to play Sunday-school teacher —a job that suits me almost as well as nuclear scientist.

"Honey, Tibbish was sick, and now Jesus is taking care of him."

"Jesus make Tibbish better?"

"Yes, son."

"Then Tibbish come back?"

"No, sweetheart. Tibbish, er, lives with Jesus now."

"TIBBISH MINE! I WANT TIBBISH! I DON'T LIKE JESUS!"

Wonderful. Earlier in the hour, my son thought Jesus was a neat guy—neater than Santa Claus, even—who took care of Mommy, Daddy, and all his friends. Now I'd convinced the boy that Jesus is someone who swipes goldfish from little kids when they aren't looking.

"Daddy, you go to Jesus's house and get Tibbish."

"Honey, I can't. Jesus lives very far away, up in the sky."

"In the sky? With Luke Skywalker?"

Yikes. "Um, sort of, I guess. Yeah."

"Daddy, you take rocket ship to Jesus's house and get Tibbish, okay?"

Obviously, my son had no difficulty imagining me storming heaven armed with a light sword and a bullhorn: "All right, Jesus! We've got you surrounded! Let the fish hostage go and come out with your hands up!"

I was down to two options. I could try to explain The Great Unknown to a three-year-old, or I could sneak out, buy another twelve-cent goldfish, slip it into the tank, and spend the rest of the day celebrating Tibbish's miraculous return from the dead.

Call it a weakness, but I find it difficult to pass up *any* twelve-cent solution.

So, a few hours later: "Honey! Look! Tibbish is back!"

"That not Tibbish. No spot. And that's a *baby.*"

"Hmmm. You know, I think you're right!" It is possible to fool some of the people some of the time; it is not possible to fool someone brighter than yourself. "Maybe Jesus brought you this fish."

"I don't want him! I want Tibbish!"

Happily for parents, even bright children have short attention spans. It wasn't long before my son started ignoring Baby just as he'd ignored Tibbish . . . until he found Baby sound asleep in the old, familiar back-float position.

"Daddy, is Jesus going to take Baby, too?"

Having learned my lesson, I explained, gently, that Baby wasn't asleep, but dead. As dead as Bambi's mother. As dead as the Wicked Witches of the East and West. As dead as Megalon the giant cockroach monster at the end of *Godzilla vs. Megalon.* Dead.

My son thought about this for a few moments, then brightened up: "Daddy, Jesus can *have* him."

Together, we removed Baby from the tank, wrapped him in a napkin, went outside, and gave him a proper burial in the garden.

MICHAEL BURKETT   To this day, my son hasn't said another word about Baby. But he still talks about rescuing Tibbish from that fishnapping Jesus character.

Say What?

It happens every day to every parent in every household in the world. You make an honest and sincere attempt to communicate with your children; you speak slowly, simply, and precisely; you repeat every-thing two or three times ... and *somehow*, nothing sinks in. They just stare at you as if you were yammering in Swahili, then continue to do exactly as they please.

What's the problem? There are six possibilities:

1. You *are* yammering in Swahili.
2. Your voice is so high-pitched it can only be heard by dogs.
3. You are insane.
4. Your kids are the victims of a mysterious disease that renders them deaf whenever you open your mouth.
5. You have died and been condemned to a particularly irritating corner of Kiddie Hell.
6. You have merely failed to realize that children do not speak the same language as adults.

If any of the first five explanations apply to you, tough luck. But if all you need to close your communications gap is a good, reliable translator, let us once again drop to our knees and thank God that I'm here to help.

How Children Interpret Key Adult Phrases

What You Say: "No!"

What They Hear: "Check with Mom for a second opinion. Then check with Grandma, Grandpa, your little sister, and the neighbors until *someone* says 'yes.'"

What You Say: "I thought I told you not to do that! Hoo, boy, you're in big trouble now!"

What They Hear: "Anyone up for a round of hide-and-seek?"

What You Say: "Look at me when I'm talking to you!"

What They Hear: "Stare into space and fiddle with your zipper until my lips stop moving."

What You Say: "Do you understand me?"

What They Hear: "Good news! My lips will stop moving any second now and you'll be able to go back to your room and play!"

What You Say: "Don't you ever, *ever* do that again!"

What They Hear: Gibberish.

What You Say: "Okay. You can go back to your room now. But don't make a mess!"

What They Hear: "Please feel free to upend as many crates of toys as you like until we can no longer locate your bed."

What You Say: "Clean up your room."

What They Hear: "Very slowly pick up one toy, look at it, forget what you were told to do, and start playing Interplanetary War."

What You Say: "Quiet down!"

What They Hear: "I'll bet you a thousand dollars you can't get loud enough to shatter glass."

What You Say: "Time to wash up for supper!"

What They Hear: "You will not be allowed to play with your friends ever again and you will die sad and alone because we're evil, sadistic parents who derive great pleasure from destroying your life and happiness. HA HA HA HA HA HA HA!"

Key Children's Phrases and What They Really Mean

What They Say: "I don't want supper! I wanna play!"

Translation: "This is your last chance to prove you're not evil, sadistic parents. Don't blow it."

What They Say: "This food is yucky!"

Translation: "I've never actually tasted this substance before, but since it doesn't appear to be loaded with sugar, I wouldn't touch it with a ten-foot fork."

What They Say: "What's for dessert?"

Translation: "Exactly how much of this crud do I have to hide under my mashed potatoes while praying you will be stricken with such a debilitating brain disease that you won't notice?"

What They Say: "Will you help me clean up my room?"

Translation: "Sorry, pal, I'm busy. If you want this mess cleaned up so badly, grab a shovel and be my guest."

What They Say: "I dunno."

Translation: "What's that? You thought I was actually *listening* to you? HA HA HA HA HA HA HA!"

What They Say: "Yes, I'm listening now."

Translation: "Let's see. As soon as his lips stop moving, I think I'll watch *Ultra-Man*, then *Beetlejuice*, then ..."

What They Say: "I love you."

Translation: The safest response to any question which might be leading to a spanking.

What They Say: "Why?"

Translation: A meaningless word that's fun to say over and over until Mom and Dad start grinding their teeth.

The Headless Robot

Parenting is like any other job. There are days when you dream of taking up a less challenging line of work, like nude lion wrestling. And there are days when you wouldn't trade places with the Royal Family's live-in wine taster.

Not so coincidentally, the best of times seem to come along when kids are doing what kids do best: helping us cynical old folks rediscover the world as they discover it for the first time, and offering handy reminders of what life was like when nothing could go wrong which optimism and imagination couldn't set right.

Granted, when you hand your children a lemon, they can whine and moan and carry on just like the rest of us. But sometimes they make lemonade. And every now and then they squeeze themselves champagne.

There was the time when my three-year-old son was playing with a cheap plastic robot—one of untold millions which litter his bedroom floor to this day. Well, during a particularly fierce bedroom battle between Godzilla, E.T., and Jabba the Hut, disaster struck. The robot's head broke off.

Let me tell you, the boy was distraught . . . for about .002 seconds. He then made a wonderful discovery.

"Daddy! Daddy!" he hollered. "Look what I've got! A headless robot!"

There he was, holding seven-tenths of a toy which had suddenly become his most prized possession. No other poseable action figure in his massive collection would *think* of messing with a robot that can kill, maim, and destroy entire planets without benefit of a head.

I tried to revive this admirable quality in myself a few days later, when a young, uninsured driver crunched a fender on my nearly new car. "Wow!" I exclaimed while surveying the damage. "Now I'll be able to tell *my* nearly new car from all the others!"

It didn't work. With age, despite what anyone may tell you, it's not your memory nor eyesight nor sex drive that's the first to go. It's your talent for making lemonade.

And that tragedy is directly followed by the loss of another precious childhood gift: zero concept of time.

I remember being faced with the awful task of telling my son that we'd have to postpone a camping trip we'd been planning for weeks. "You mean...we're not...goin' camping?" he said in much the same tone a child might ask, "You mean...you're gonna...kill my kitten?"

"No, sweetheart," I replied. "We're still going camping. But not Friday. We'll have to go another day."

I expected a small fit. Instead, my tent-partner-to-be raced straight to his mother. "Mommy! Mommy! Guess what? Me and Daddy are going camping *another day!*"

To a preschooler who doesn't know the difference between 2 P.M. this afternoon and October 1999, "another day" could arrive *before* Friday. Heck, it could come along at any minute. What could be more exciting than that?

That's the third item to fail on us oldsters: the ability to get pumped up and goggle-eyed over an indefinite camping trip, a helicopter, a full moon, a spider's web, even a trip to the mailbox.

I used to dread making the quarter-mile hike required to collect our mail because I was grown-up enough to suspect that more bad news than good awaited me. Yet whenever my son tags along, drudgery becomes adventure.

"Maybe there's mail for me!" he always says while scrambling onto his tricycle. "Maybe a postcard. Or a magazine. Or a present. Maybe. We'll see."

When his optimism pays off, he beams as if he'd just knocked the head off another plastic robot. And when it doesn't?

"Oh, well," he shrugs, remounting his three-wheeled hawg. "Maybe I'll get mail another day."

Curse of the Night Demon

Bedtime for Bonzo, Jr.

A Compelling True-Life
Sci-Fi Docudrama in 11 Acts

Act One

(It is 9 P.M. As the curtain rises, the large, bearded man is tucking the small, unbearded boy into bed.)

BOY: Daddy, will you read me a book? Pleeeease? One book? A small book?

MAN: All right. If you promise to stay in bed afterward. Do you promise?

BOY: I promise.

MAN: Which book do you want me to read?

BOY: *The King of the Space Vampires.*

MAN: Absolutely not. You know Mommy has forbidden you to read that book until you're thirty-six.

BOY: Oh, yeah. Well, how about . . . ummmm . . . let's see . . . I know! How about . . . uhhh . . . how about . . . read me a story about . . . I've got a good idea! Why don't you read me the story about . . . ummm . . . How about . . . ahhh . . . Hey! Let's read . . .

MAN: Forget it. We're reading the first book I find in this pile . . .

Act Two

(9:20 P.M.)

MAN: . . . and just as the King of the Space Vampires was about to sink his fangs into Princess Lorelei's neck, Zor-Ack fired his laser-Uzi and transformed the horribly disfigured bloodsucker into a puddle of radioactive goop. The universe was saved, and everyone who hadn't been sucked dry lived happily ever after. The end.

BOY: A lot of people die in that book. I like it.

Act Three

(9:26 P.M.)

MAN: I thought you promised to stay in bed.

BOY: I heard a noise outside.

MAN: Of course you did. There are people and cars and all sorts of things that make noise outside.

BOY: Maybe it's the King of the Space Vampires.

MAN: Couldn't be. He was turned into radioactive goop. Remember?

BOY: Oh, yeah.

Act Four

(9:27 P.M.)

BOY: Maybe it's Freddy Krueger.

MAN: Freddy Krueger isn't real. He's just pretend.

BOY: Not when you're sleeping.

Act Five

(9:28 P.M.)

BOY: Daddy?

MAN: What NOW?

BOY: You forgot to brush my teeth.

Act Six

(9:31 P.M.)

BOY: I gotta pee.

Act Seven

(9:35 P.M.)

BOY: I think my leg is broken.

MAN: In that case, you'll have to go to the doctor and stay in bed for a long, long time.

BOY: It's better now.

Act Eight

(9:38 p.m.)

BOY: I'm thirsty.

Act Nine

(9:43 p.m.)

BOY: Daddy, I have to ask you something. Something important. Something very, very important. Dad . . . Dad . . . Dad . . . Dad . . .

MAN: What?!?!?

BOY: Maybe the King of the Space Vampires turned into the Blob and now instead of just sucking your blood he eats your whole body.

Act Ten

(9:46 p.m.)

MAN: *Get back in bed right now!*

BOY: Daddy, I think I'm sick.

MAN: *You're not sick!*

BOY: I think I'm gonna throw up.

MAN: Then throw up while you're getting back in bed! (The boy throws up.)

MICHAEL
BURKETT

Act Eleven

(11:38 P.M. Father and son are in the living room watching "The Love Connection." Mommy enters.)

MOMMY: What are you doing up at this hour, young man?

BOY: Daddy made me.

(Blackout. Curtain. Scream.)

Gender Bender

I don't know why so many expectant parents race to the nearest ultrasound machine the moment their fetus is old enough to announce its gender. As far as I'm concerned, not knowing exactly what you're going to get is half the fun of preparenting.

(The other half occurred during my wife's final week of hugeness, when she couldn't extract herself from a broom closet. But that's another column. Or perhaps another book.)

I have always liked the fact that Cracker Jack boxes say "Surprise Inside!" rather than "Laughably Cheap, Tiny, Plastic Magnifying Glass Inside!" For the same reason, I enjoyed not knowing until the messy moment of truth whether my newest relative was a future president of the United States or a future beauty-queen-turned-president-of-the-United States.

Well, actually, there wasn't *that* much suspense, because the same instinctive voice that tells me to eat, breathe, breed, and avoid "America's Funniest Home Videos" kept whispering, "It's a girl! It's a girl!"

My wife received identical mental bulletins. And apparently, so did everyone we met. Complete strangers would eye the mass that was once her waistline and conclude, "You're carrying the baby high. That means it's a girl." Others would say, "You're carrying the baby low. That means it's a girl." Still others would declare, "If you carry a baby high or low, it's a boy. Yours is right in the middle. It's a girl."

Usually, these freelance psychics were thrilled for us—but not always. During my wife's sixth or seventh trimester (it was a loooong pregnancy), we vacationed in Jamaica, where it is considered a sign of incredible good fortune if your firstborn is male.

"I'm so sorry," one islander said after sizing us up as definite girl-makers. "Perhaps you will find happiness in your lives at any rate."

While this woman surely intended to console us, her tentative delivery of the word "perhaps" made it clear we'd be lucky if we weren't attacked by swarms of rabid, plague-infested bats on the way home from the hospital.

Back home we consulted our Ouija board, which spelled out "It's a girl." We then consulted one of those fortune-telling eight-balls for a second-hundredth opinion: "Trust your instincts." Just to be safe, we returned to the Ouija board. "Trust the eight-ball," it told us.

So we *knew*.

To cover all our bases, we spent about three-and-a-half seconds dickering over what we'd name the kid if it turned out to be a (snicker, snicker) boy. For the remainder of the pregnancy, we wrestled with girl's names. Day and night.

Taking a shower, I'd suddenly scream, "Rachel!"

"No way!" my wife would holler back. "I knew a Rachel in the fourth grade. She was a creep with ringworm who always shook her head over our open lunchboxes. How about 'Rebecca'?"

"Absolutely not. That was the name of the first girl I ever danced with. We danced the Mashed Potato. The little snob is probably *still* laughing at the memory. Let's name her Kim."

"Ptooey! All the Kims I ever knew were cheerleaders."

You never realize how many people you've hated over the years until you try to name a kid.

We didn't come to an agreement on the matter until my wife gave her final delivery-room push and screamed, "KATE!"

Yep. That was the perfect name, all right. And it remained perfect all the way to the official medical proclamation, "Congratulations. Looks like you've got yourselves a boy."

Clearly, a grave error had been made. But how? I'd heard of hospitals accidentally switching babies, although I'd never heard of it happening so early. I mean, the umbilical cord was still attached! Even the most absent-minded medicos would have a hard time losing track of a baby that was still connected to its mother.

I promptly inspected the kid, hoping to find a strawberry birthmark or some other clue that might tip us off to the identity of his real parents (who were no doubt oohing and ahhing over my missing daughter at that very moment). That's when my inner voice said, "This is your son."

"Heyyyy, wait a minute," I thought. "Could this be the same inner voice that's been blithering, 'It's a girl, it's a girl'?"

"Correct," the voice replied. "And aren't you the same guy who likes the fact that Cracker Jack boxes say 'Surprise Inside'?"

That was me, all right.

Now, I can look back on all the Cracker Jack boxes I've ever emptied and say that I've rarely found a niftier "Surprise Inside" than my son. Heck, I wouldn't trade him for a *dozen* cheap, tiny, plastic magnifying glasses.

Take it from me. Forget the ultrasound machine and trust your instincts. Even if you catch 'em lying through your teeth.

Cheap Tricks

According to a recent national study, the cost of raising a child up to age eighteen ranges from about $54,000 per poor child to $145,000 for those of the well-to-do variety.

Now that those figures have been released, the demand for poor kids is certain to skyrocket. But the fact of the matter is, child rearing can actually be a *profitable* venture. All you need is a little common sense.

For the nonce, feel free to borrow mine.

Day-Care: Why dump thousands of dollars into lousy day-care when you can get lousy day-care *absolutely free?* On your way to work, stop off at the corner supermarket. Tell the manager you've found a lost child, point to your kid, and beat a hasty retreat. By the time you return—sobbing hysterically over your "missing baby"—the store's day manager will have been replaced by the evening manager. No one will be the wiser.

After a while you may get a reputation for being terribly absent-minded, but so what? You'll be laughing all the way to the bank. Possible savings per child: $22,000.

Toys: What do toddlers love most about birthdays and Christmas? Pricey designer-label playthings that go completely ignored or break within hours? No. More than anything, they love romping in piles of giftwrap, ribbons, and empty boxes—the gift that keeps on giving. Take advantage of this phenomenon while it lasts. Possible savings per child: $36,850.

Clothing: There are few holidays children enjoy more than Halloween. So quit dropping hefty chunks of income on conventional duds and let your kid dress up as a new "character" every day! The list of fun, zip-budget costume ideas is endless: hobo, match girl, ghetto child, nudist, cardboard-box robot, etc. Possible savings per child: $42,000.

Housing: It's your choice. You can cash out on a bigger home to accommodate your growing family...or you can capitalize on the young American's inborn love of adventure and the great outdoors by erecting a tent in your backyard. Or just hammer a stick into the ground and throw an old sheet over it; your child's imagination will do the rest.

Not only will you be helping to develop the kid's pioneering spirit, your neighbors (or at least those under the age of nine) will think you're the coolest parent in the universe. Possible savings per child: $63,000.

Allowances: It is of utmost importance to teach youngsters the value of a dollar. So give your child a dollar. Then tell him it's the last

free cash he'll see until he wins the lottery, lucks out on a TV game show, or successfully contests your will. Possible savings per child: $38,000.

Family Vacations: Last summer, we took a one-week trip to Disneyland, Sea World, and the San Diego Zoo. When my son wasn't whining, crying, or behaving like Bomba the Jungle Boy, he was upchucking $3.50 hot dogs.

This summer, we vacationed in the mountains, fifty-five minutes from home. My son spent the week throwing rocks into a creek and dining on thirty-five cent campfire-roasted hot dogs. He had a great time. So did I. There's a lesson to be learned here—not to mention a possible savings of $16,000 per child.

Education: It's fine to want to bestow the rewards of higher education on your children. But before you dump your life savings into that dream, consider these sobering statistics:

Out of every ten students enrolled in college, nine goof off; three read a lightly or nonillustrated book in its entirety; one remembers the title; seven drop out before graduation; two earn useless degrees; one gets a degree in a potentially lucrative but hopelessly overcrowded profession and ultimately finds work as a grade-school crosswalk guard; and all ten become huge disappointments to their families.

Conversely, out of every ten youths who do not attend college, ten goof off—but only eight become huge disappointments to their families (usually when they break parole). Possible savings per child: $125,000.

Medical Care: A high-ticket item, to be sure. But luckily, the billing departments of most medical institutions are staffed by idiots. Either 1) your child's records will be lost forever, 2) you'll receive someone else's bill, 3) you'll be outrageously overcharged for services rendered, or 4) you'll be outrageously overcharged for services they made up and tacked on to your bill just for the fun of it.

Whatever the case, send them an indignant letter. They will reply with an incomprehensible letter (no doubt composed by a former college student). This back-and-forth correspondence can be stretched out for years. By the time everyone agrees on who owes what to whom, your pride and joy will be old enough to assume responsibility for his or her own debts. Possible savings per child: $700,500.

If you've been following along with a calculator, you're aware that these simple, cost-cutting ideas could save single-child parents enough money to sire an additional 1,173 poor children or 587 well-to-do children . . . and still break even!

Don't mention it. I'm here to help.

Bribe and Groom

Two long-time friends recently decided to get married after seventeen years of dating. How this could happen in America is beyond me. But it did.

The wedding was to be a major northern California to-do, attended by some two hundred of the bride and groom's most intimate intimates, many of whom would be flying in from all corners of the country.

To the guests, this was The Event of the Century. I don't think any of us believed the gala ceremony would actually take place, but it was worth showing up to hear one or the other of the marrieds-to-be cop an eleventh-hour plea.

So suspense was in the air. But nowhere—apart from the bride and groom's respective digs—could it have been as thick as it was at my house, where my three-year-old son was being prepped to play the crucial role of ringbearer.

The ringbearer's responsibilities are not overwhelming. He simply walks down the aisle, hands the ring to the best man, stands silently and mannequin-still for fifteen or twenty minutes, poses for a few group photos, and is then congratulated by one and all for the fine job he's done.

That's how it's supposed to go, anyway. Unfortunately, my son has never been one to stick to a script. I could easily envision him flying down the aisle, screaming like a wounded pterodactyl (his favorite animal impression); losing the ring; upstaging the stars with a fifteen-

or twenty-minute fit; making the photographer wish he were shooting a Middle Eastern battle zone for *Time* magazine; driving the newlyweds to a speedy annulment; and effectively destroying The Event of the Century.

Were that to happen, of course, no one could blame him. He's only three. He's *supposed* to have the attention span of the South American newt (which has been known to starve to death because it forgot it had food in its mouth).

It's normal. Just like his usual response to the threat "If you throw your tricycle at Bradley *one more time,* you're going straight to bed" —which is to promptly throw his tricycle at Bradley. On the way to the bedroom you ask, "Why did you throw your tricycle at Bradley when I told you not to?"

"I forgot."

"Well, the next time you forget, your bike is going in the garbage. Okay?"

"Okay."

"Now tell me what I just said."

"You said . . . um . . . ahh . . . you said no dessert if I'm bad."

"That is *not* what I said. *Tell me what I said."*

"You said . . . you said . . . um . . . Daddy?"

"What?"

"I love you."

See? He's an average kid. I had no reason to believe he *wouldn't* screw up The Event of the Century.

During the wedding rehearsal, our little ringbearer made it all the way down the aisle without unbearing himself of the ring—but then demonstrated that he was not about to stand silently and mannequin-still for any period of time whatsoever.

Thankfully, he was relieved of that duty. Upon delivery of the goods to the best man, he was to come sit next to Mommy and Daddy.

We rehearsed. All the way home and all the way back to the church the next day:

"All right. What are you going to do with the ring?"

"I told you already!"

"Tell me again."

"I'm gonna carry the ring and give it to Uncle Dana."

"No, not Uncle Dana. *Uncle David.*"

"Yeah. Uncle David."

"And then what?"

"Sit with Mommy and Daddy."

"Very good. Excellent. Now, once more. What are you going do with the ring?"

"I TOLD YOU ALREADY..."

To further ensure a flawless performance, we offered a bribe. It's a sad truth and not one you like to think applies to your own flesh and blood, but a child's love, obedience, and attention can be bought. And the price you name is in direct proportion to the amount of love, obedience, and attention he will dispense.

A ninety-nine-cent Hot Wheels roadster, for example, will get you approximately three minutes of love, obedience, and attention, whereas a twelve-dollar wind-up, walking dinosaur skeleton can buy you up to a half-hour's worth—if the child is well-napped, fully fed, and not in wound-up prehistoric-monster mode himself.

Just as The Event of the Century was about to unfold, we showed him the twelve-dollar wind-up, walking dinosaur skeleton and promised it would be his, forever, if he ever came through for Mommy and Daddy. After one more quick rehearsal: "I TOLD YOU ALREADY!", we abandoned him to take our seats.

The bagpipes started playing (a mere organ would not suffice for The Event of the Century), and the wedding procession began. There came the groom, the best man, the flower girl...and my son, whose entrance elicited two hundred "Awwwwwws" that sounded like a thousand in the cavernous church.

At that moment I realized why parents don't hang up on friends looking for three-year-old ringbearers. They don't hang up because they know in their heart of hearts that their child is ridiculously adorable and that, given the chance, the world would agree with a sweet, gentle chorus of "Awwwwwwws." And even if the world *didn't* agree, Mommy and Daddy would be too busy wiping away tears of pride to notice.

Although it suddenly seemed unimportant, my son handed the ring to Uncle David, not Uncle Dana, and scurried off to sit with his beaming parents, precisely as directed.

Sensing the formality of the occasion, he spoke to us in a whisper: *"Okay. I did it. Now where's my dinosaur skeleton?"*

The crowd was so awestruck by the lad's performance that nobody seemed to mind that he refused to part with his hard-earned booty when it came time to pose for the wedding-party photos.

In the future, when historians look closely at photographic records of The Event of the Century, they will see a small boy off to the side, disassembling a twelve-dollar wind-up, walking dinosaur skeleton.

That's my son. Awwwwww.

Parent Peeves

I love being a dad. But the job is not without certain details that make me want to remove my clothes, climb City Hall, and do birdcalls until I'm hauled off to some nice, safe place where I can't hurt myself.

For example:

Plastic-Strip Thermometers: These space-age devices make swell bookmarks and are very helpful in removing food that's lodged between your teeth. As thermometers, however, they're worthless—except in cases where all you need to determine is the vague probability that Junior's temperature is somewhere between 62 and 136 degrees.

Juice in a Box: Surely another fine product from the zanies who brought us plastic-strip thermometers. These "convenient" little cardboard containers remain convenient until you are forced to hammer the accompanying straw through the steel-reinforced aluminum siding that covers the straw hole. That's when the juice (usually some perma-stain flavor like grape, cranberry, or grape-cranberry) squirts all over your shirt. And then, when your kid so much as *touches* the box, it squirts all over his shirt, the furniture, the carpet, the car upholstery, the cat, and the neighborhood kids. Lawsuits ensue.

Toy Prices: Hey. I don't mind buying my son's affections. But for this kind of money, I could buy Cindy Crawford's affections.

Toy Commercials: The way I figure it, what my boy doesn't know he doesn't own won't hurt him. Well, thanks to the reminders and updates he gets every three minutes on TV, he knows. And he's threatening to leave home unless he gets *all of it* for his birthday.

Toy Packaging: Step One: Your child beams as you hand him a two-by-three-foot box for Christmas. Step Two: He opens the box, finds three ounces of plastic and five pounds of Styrofoam that cost you $29.95, and just *knows* you've kept all the good stuff for yourself.

Playing Simon "Daddy" Legree: Your son waits hours for his neighbor pal to come home from preschool. When his neighbor pal finally returns, ready to play like he's never played before, you're the one who gets to step outside and announce, "Time to wash up for supper!"

Imitation Suicide: This natural phenomenon occurs when you've ordered your child to perform some unthinkably horrible task (i.e., washing up for supper just when his neighbor pal has come home). In between caterwauls, your kid appears to stop breathing. And just when you're ready to see how much you *really* learned in CPR class, he starts screaming again. This cycle can repeat for hours.

Disposable Diaper Tape: Here's another good reason to rid the world of disposable diapers. If you sprinkle baby powder within a half-mile radius of 'em, the tape won't stick. The diaper is now useless. But it costs too much to throw away. So you spend the next twenty minutes looking for something that will hold it together, like rivets or a soldering gun. To no avail. So you throw the diaper away and start all over. This cycle can repeat for hours.

Kiddie Air Fares: I don't get it. A plane ticket for a forty-pound kid who doesn't know where he's going or care if he comes back costs *exactly* as much as a ticket for a three-hundred-pound adult with a specific destination in mind.

Music Boxes, Stuffed Animals, Greeting Cards and Anything Else That Plays "It's a Small World": I swear. I am not a violent man. But let's kill the guy who wrote that song. Okay?

Coming Attractions: You take your kid to the only G-rated movie to hit town in months. Prior to the main feature, he's treated to previews for *Sorority House Bloodbath, The Arkansas Electric-Screwdriver*

MICHAEL BURKETT *Massacre* and *Terminator IV: The Disemboweling.* Then you've got to deal with his disappointment when he finds out he's there to see *Pinnochio Goes to Candyland.*

Killer Instincts

As a child of the sixties
Who was into love and peace,
It, like, wow, man, really bummed me
To see global strife increase.
So I long ago decided,
If I ever had some sons,
That never would I buy them
Any war toys, any guns.

That's a vow I stuck to
Once I finally had a boy;
Never have we given him
A weapon for a toy.
But what I failed to count on
Was a young lad's innate knack
For wanting to do nothing more
Than search, destroy, *attack!*

We first got him a rattle,
But we had to trash it quick
When he used it as a blackjack
The next Christmas, on Saint Nick.
And then he got a teething ring;
No harm in that at all ...

MICHAEL
BURKETT

Until we caught him garroting
His cousin's Barbie doll.

Soon all sticks were viewed as swords;
The short ones used as knives
(Two of them made nunchakus,
Which are swell for taking lives).
Marbles made great bullets,
And balls, bazooka shells.
Play-Doh made explosive clay
To blow things all to hell.

Now that my son is in first grade,
The problem still persists;
This boy can make a weapon
Out of anything you list.
Not just toys and playthings,
But *any* random stuff,
Becomes to him a handy tool
To torture, maim, and snuff.

Give this boy a lemon,
He will not make lemonade;
Instead that citrus will become
A deadly hand grenade.
Or barbecue a hot dog;
He'll remove it from the bun
And spray the house with rapid fire;
It's an all-beef tommy gun!

Of all the errors that we've made,
The biggest one as yet
Was when we gave our little man

A harmless Lego set.
In no time he constructed
A complete munitions center,
Within an eight-foot fortress
Audie Murphy couldn't enter.

Safe inside, he built himself
Twelve full-size flame projectors;
Rifles, cannons, howitzers
And fireball ejectors;
Browning automatics,
Smith and Wesson .37s,
Each with bayonets attached,
From one up to eleven.

When I hollered, "This is it!
Get out of there right now!"
The boy just laughed a wicked laugh
And dusted a stuffed cow.
"I'm going in!" I told my wife,
As flak whizzed past my knee.
"You stay here. Protect yourself.
And for God's sake, cover me!"

Dodging crayon missles,
And antiaircraft blocks,
And rockets made of Golden Books,
And land mines made of socks,
I hit the wall with all my might
And damned near blackened out.
"Ha ha! Good try! But no cigar!"
I heard the monster shout.

**MICHAEL
BURKETT**

The boy's assault continued from
Ten-thirty till past three.
That's when the perfect, foolproof plan
At long last came to me.
"Son, it's almost three o'clock,"
I yelled out through the noise.
"It's time to watch your cartoon faves,
'The Barnyard Death-Squad Boys'!

"After that comes 'Toxic Ninja
Sniper Slugs at War,'
And then 'Guerilla Bunnies
And the Psycho-Killer Corps,'
Followed next by that kid show
You really, truly love,
'Stark-Crazy Sociopathic
Flying Chipmunks from Above.'"

44

Suddenly, the shooting stopped!
The smoke began to clear!
A white flag raised above the fort
Said, yes, the end was here.
Sonny scampered from his bunker
and ran toward the TV set
To watch his favorite programs;
He has never missed them yet.

That left me with some quiet time
To contemplate and wonder
Where my son learned that it's fun
to kill, destroy, and plunder.
From whence he got this notion

Well, I haven't got a clue.
It must come from Mother Nature,
Not from anything I do.

Dog Daze

The facts have been hushed up for over thirty years due to a provision in Walt Disney's will. However, you are about to learn the *real* reason Dorothy McGuire made Tommy Kirk shoot Old Yeller, and rabies had nothing to do with it.

But first, let me present the shocking educational printumentary, "Selecting a Child's First Dog: One Parent's Nightmare."

As far as all-American pairings go, A Boy and His Dog is right up there with Love and Marriage, Soup and Sandwich, and Death and Taxes. So naturally, when my son began to appreciate the difference between pets and building blocks, I began drafting a list of the qualifications any canine would have to meet to become a member of our happy family unit.

1.   He would have to be at least a year old. I'm too old to go through puppy-training again; too old to step barefooted into warm surprises; too old to find humor in the sight of my favorite belongings chewed to soggy smithereens. And besides, it takes about one year for a dog's true personality to emerge. Ignore this fact and one day, there you'll be, fresh out of Jerky Treats and cornered in your own kitchen by Cujo the Devil-Dog from Hell.

2.   He must be lap-sized. Our house is so small, cluttered, and yardless that the only free space we have is in our laps. If we ever have any more kids, they'll have to be lap-sized, too. And they'll have to stay that way until we can afford to move.

3. Mellow. Better yet, narcoleptic. Actually, what I really had in mind was all the symptoms of death except rigor mortis and decay.

My standards set, I immediately made my first mistake. My wife said, "Say! Let's see what we can find at the animal shelter," and I said —I *still* can't believe it—"Okay, dear."

Important rule: A visit to the animal shelter should never be turned into a fun family outing, unless your family is riddled with sadists and masochists. The place is as uplifting as an orphan's funeral and not at all conducive to sane, unemotional decision-making.

As a rule, animal shelters are populated by four types of dogs: runaways, the abandoned, the psychotic, and the quarantined. None are ideal adoption material. Take home a runaway, for example, and he'll run away. Take home an abandoned dog, and you're sure to find he was abandoned for good reason. Psychotic dogs are fine until you do something foolish, like make eye contact or try to pet them. Then they become quarantined dogs.

A further problem is that any dog with only a few hours to live automatically takes on the most adorable characteristics of a puppy. It's astounding. I'm sure John Wayne Gacy is no more adorable now than when he was digging up his yard. But a pit bull who's set to die for eating a family of six? *He's* adorable.

So was the mutt we finally chose to rescue from Doggy Death Row. The one my son named Buddy.

It wasn't until we got Buddy out to the car that I realized he was much bigger and younger than he'd seemed inside. And it wasn't until I read the paperwork that I realized we'd adopted a seven-month-old Border collie—a breed with no use for a human lap. If you have sixty acres and a few hundred head of sheep in need of herding, you get yourself a Border collie.

But what the hey. My son was ecstatic. He had a dog who looked just like Benji. If you stood back a few hundred yards and squinted reeeeeal hard.

Once home, I opened the door, removed Buddy's leash, and said something gracious like, "Welcome to your new home!" Within twelve minutes the dog soaked the couch, fouled my slippers, mistook a videocassette for a rawhide chew toy, howled whenever we left the room, and knocked my son down with an overly affectionate greeting whenever we returned.

It was around the thirteenth minute that my boy decided he didn't want a dog after all. So he took it very well when Buddy—apparently a former runaway—ran away.

Honest. I did not aid his escape. I simply opened the door to admit a visitor, and at a speed exceeding any ever attained by Chuck Yeager, Buddy was gone. Out of the house, neighborhood, and perhaps the state.

After a long, fruitless search, I took my son aside and broke the horrible news.

"Oh," he said, remarkably dry-eyed. Then panic struck. "Dad . . . we're not gonna get *another* dog, are we?"

Five days later, I was certain Buddy had become one with a Buick. Imagine my surprise when I came home and found him chained to the kitchen table—which he'd upended and dragged into the living room, knocking over the stereo along the way.

Seems some well-meaning folks halfway across town had found him and run a lost-and-found ad ("Black/white Border collie, unhousebroken and energetic") that my wife happened to see.

Oooh, what luck.

I thought of borrowing Dorothy McGuire's rabies story, thinking my son would be happy to reenact the Tommy Kirk role. But eventually I concluded that even the dumbest of God's animals has the right to live—provided they do it at somebody else's house. Like my in-laws.

My wife's parents possess many fine qualities, but the finest is that they continually make grand offers without seeming to worry you may accept. And when Buddy returned, they made their grandest offer yet: "We have a big yard. He can live with us."

If Dorothy McGuire had such big-hearted relatives, she wouldn't have had to invent her rabies cover-up story or fork out for a shotgun. And *Old Yeller* would have ended on the upbeat, like this story. Buddy's happy, my wife is happy, even my in-laws are happy.

Oh, yes. My son is happy, too. Except when we're at Grandma's house and someone tells him to go out back and play with his dog.

Moniker Madness

Every day, newspaper headlines scream of crimes against children. Yet there is one rampant horror you never read about. Its victims are helpless newborns, and it destroys their lives.

Fact: Every twenty-six seconds in this country, a child is born with an idiotic name.

Why the government hasn't stepped in, I don't know. But it's got to stop. The world is tough enough without a birth certificate that identifies you as "Cinnamon Schwartz," "Autumn Sternhagen," or "Lance Boyle."

Not long ago, my wife and I were in the lobby of a Los Angeles theater when we heard someone behind us say, "Bob, I'd like you to meet Buffy."

Naturally, we laughed. Derisively and out loud. Buffy?!? That's a name for a cat or a golden retriever or a hamster, not a human being. Hang a label like that on a kid, and you might as well plug a neon sign into her forehead that flashes "Loser! Loser!" Her life will peak when she makes the high school cheerleading team. Then, if she's lucky, she'll marry the star quarterback, pump out a half-dozen badly named kids, and be trapped in her own laundry room until she ODs on tranquilizers and alcohol. All because her parents had the poor taste and lack of foresight to name her Buffy.

I spun around to get a load of the Buffy behind us. As it turned out, it was Buffy Sainte-Marie, the renowned American Indian folksinger —and the only person on earth who can get away with being called Buffy.

But the point remains: Do not gamble with your daughter's life and happiness by naming her Buffy. And don't name your son Buffy, either. The chances that he or she will mature into a renowned American Indian folksinger are perilously slim.

It's astonishing how the sanity of thoughtful, loving, rational parents can snap under the pressure of baby-naming. I once read an interview with William Lear, the late zillionaire developer of the Lear jet. Of all his accomplishments, Lear bragged, he was proudest of his daughters. Their names, if memory serves, are Chanda Lear, Cava Lear, and Gonda Lear.

Now, it's one thing to inflict your poor taste on innocent babies. But to punish them for your dismal sense of humor is quite another. The Lear case is the only one I can think of where three children in the same family would have been better off with the name Buffy.

What we need, desperately, are federally appointed Name Police; armed and uniformed guardians of the aesthetic appellative, legally required to be present at all births and empowered to mete out justice to anyone who even thinks of saddling his kid with a moronic moniker.

Offenders would be deemed a menace to society, and their reproductive organs would be removed on the spot—manually, without anesthesia. Or, to really teach 'em a lesson, their first and middle names would be legally changed to "Moonbeam Starlight."

Until civilization advances to that point, we must take it upon ourselves to draw up some basic baby-naming no-nos:

No puns (i.e., Hedda Hare), echoes (William Williams), rhymes (Ernie McGurney), clever word plays (Jack Anjill), alliterations (Kristie, Kirstie, and Krusty Kesselman), or names that would take on whole new meanings when reversed in the phone book (Dick Little).

No names borrowed from foods (Sage, Muffin), seasons (Autumn, Summer), weather conditions (Sunshine, Rain, Sleet), nature (River, Leaf, Squirrelly), astrology (Star, Aquarius), rocks (Sapphire, Turquoise), celebrities (Englebert, Charo, Zsa Zsa, Liberace, Pee-wee, Soupy), rock stars (Prince, Sting, Meatloaf), sports figures (Yogi, Kareem), or fictional characters from cartoons (Bambi, Goofy), children's songs (Rudolph, Frosty), soap operas (Sable, Patch, Slut) and light operas (Porgy).

If you're the creative type, take pride that you've created a kid and leave it at that. Don't burden your heir with something new and original to make him stand out. Kids don't want to stand out. Until they're teenagers, of course, at which time they'll have learned to hate any name you've given them and will start introducing themselves by a stupid name of their own invention.

Finally, if your last name doesn't blend well with any first name, be a sport. Change it.

That's certainly the course of action I'd have recommended to Mr. and Mrs. Pugh (pronounced "Pew"), producers of one of my dishier schoolmates, Ramona Pugh. Despite her beauty, even Ramona's best friends couldn't say her name without pinching their noses and adding rude accents that turned it into "Ramona? PEE-YOO!!!"

I'd always assumed that poor Ramona couldn't wait to get married and put an end to the Ramona? Pee-yoo!!! jokes. But she eventually wed a fellow named Steve Stench, and last I heard, she was going by the hyphenated handle, "Ramona? Pee-yoo! STENCH!!!"

May God, or the Name Police, help her children.

Birth Mirth

Well, look at that! It's turning purple!"

Those were the words that changed my life. Completely.

For anyone unfamiliar with baby-making in the near-twenty-first century, the modern mother-to-be can verify her condition almost anywhere she happens to be. She simply whizzes (or whatever feminine thing it is that women do) into a vial and waits. If the stuff turns purple—as my wife's did, on the freeway, a half-hour into our vacation —life changes. Completely.

"Nah, that isn't purple," said I, ever the optimist, nearly careening into a disabled semi. "It's more of an off-violet. A semi-magenta. A burnt fuschia..."

"No, it's definitely purple," countered my bride, ever the realist. "Look. Purple just doesn't get more purple than that."

She was right. And the longer I looked at it, the purpler it got. Meanwhile, my old life passed before my eyes: over three decades of bachelorhood, loneliness, meaningless relationships, fear of responsibility, dread of commitment.

Ah, nostalgia.

Don't misunderstand. I've always been crazy about kids. We'd planned to have one. But I'm an average guy. The kind who knows exactly what he wants until it's too late to change his mind.

Now, I haven't figured out much about female synapses, but I do know they aren't soothed by male wishy-washiness toward babies— particularly when the deed, or seed, is done. So I mustered a cool demeanor and somehow kept it mustered all the way to the maternity ward, all the way to the literal "plop!" with which my first-born made his debut, all the way to the moment he was handed to me.

Naturally, he was purple.

Following the requisite oohs and aahs and new-dad blitherings, I thought, Geez. If he's this messy now, what's his room gonna look like in thirteen years? And then every fear I'd feared for 8.5 months proceeded to chill my spine:

• Please, God. Don't turn this beautiful, perfect, fully equipped child into a teenager. Don't give him a deeply flawed sense of fashion or disconnect his brain and compel him to loiter zombie-like in malls and convenience-store parking lots. PUH-LEASE! I'll do anything.

• Uh-oh. What if he grows up into someone I don't like? I've met ten thousand people in my lifetime, and there've been damn few of 'em I'd want to live with for eighteen years. Let alone buy their clothes, feed them, do their homework, accompany them to traffic court, and lend them money I'll never see again.

• What if he doesn't like me? The same odds apply. Either way, you can bet he'll never loan me money.

• He could still be living with us when he's forty! I'll be seventy-five. Or dead. Frankly, death sounds far more appealing than the prospect of telling a middle-aged bum to clean his room, get a job, and find a girl.

• Say he matures into a hopelessly miserable human being, forever traumatized when I refused to buy him his own chain of toy stores. How does a parent cope with that kind of guilt?

• Even worse, he could metamorphose into the type of village idiot commonly found behind the counters of fast-food joints. You make a ninety-seven-cent purchase, hand the kid a dollar, and his sole functioning brain cell locks up on him. He has to call the manager over to figure out your change. Oh, please, noooo!

• Then again, better a village idiot than a "loner." That's someone

who goes off the deep end and chops his family into Human Mc-
Nuggets. When the neighbors are asked to describe him on the six
o'clock news, they always say, "He's a quiet kid. Always kept to himself. A loner." If my kid ever acted like a loner, I'd never let him out
of his room. I'd make him be a loner all by himself.

• Then again, better a loner than a Young Republican...

Odd. The longer I held this tiny, screaming, purplish kid, the more
it seemed that no mistake had been made. Maybe my life was changing for the better!

Just to be safe, though, I tried to talk my wife into black-marketing
the kid and buying a parakeet. But no go. You know women. Load 'em
up with drugs, make 'em scream through twelve hellish hours of labor,
then hand 'em a loud, seven-pound fourteen-ounce replica of Fatty
Arbuckle and they lose all concept of reality.

55

Party Animal

Here, in all their pure, unexpurgated horror, are the three ugliest words a parent can hear after accepting a dinner-party invitation:

"Grandma can't babysit."

If just reading that sentence doesn't soak your Fruit of the Looms in cold sweat, you either don't have a preschooler, Grandma lives in Guam, or you're never invited to dinner parties.

Otherwise, what those words mean is that you're going to have to take your kid with you. And what *that* means is that the evening *and* your reputation as a fun couple are about to be destroyed.

By definition, dinner-party hosts don't like children and have none of their own. If they did, they'd be too tired and cranky to host dinner parties, and their homes would be too messy to allow anyone past the front door. But when such folks request the pleasure of a parent's company, their invitations traditionally conclude with, "Oh, yes, and your child is welcome to come along, too."

All dinner-party hosts say this so they'll seem like thoughtful, accommodating human beings. In truth, however, they don't want you to bring your kid any more than they want you to show up at their house with the wild coyote you captured on your last camping trip.

Nor do they *expect* you to arrive with Junior in tow. Their offer is just one of those pleasant conversation-enders people always use but never mean, like "Let's do lunch." Or "If you need help moving, give me a call." Or "Honest, I really like your new hairdo. I really, really do."

And frankly, who can blame them? While children can provide an adult with fine company in a variety of settings, out in public is not among them.

Tell a three-year-old boy he's going to a party and he'll squeal with delight—all the way to the car and all the way to the host's front porch. In fact, his excitement level won't taper off until the door opens and your hosts say something rude or threatening like, "Well, hello there! Nice to see you!"

Sometimes it happens, sometimes it doesn't—but when you most hope it *won't,* the boy will stare these strangers right in the eye and announce, "I don't like these people. I don't like this house. I wanna go home."

On such occasions, parents are compelled to make up some excuse as to why the child they've always bragged about is behaving like an honor student from the Godzilla School of Etiquette. A common fall-back position is, "Gosh, I don't know what's gotten into him. He never acts this way."

This tactic rarely works for a couple of reasons. One, the host will suspect you're lying. Two, there *will* be another guest in attendance who has met your child before, and who will be happy to refresh your memory.

Here's how I handle this situation. I take the party giver aside and whisper, "The poor kid. His dog just died." This makes your child seem more sensitive than monstrous. For a while.

Of course, all illusions shatter when the evening's bill of fare is trotted out: fresh vegetable hors d'oeuvres, leek soup, spinach salad, and eggplant parmigiana. In other words, the same menu offered at the McDonald's franchise in hell.

"I don't like this yucky food," my son would report.

"Oooooh, nooooo! It's yummy, yummy, *yummy!*" I would reply, suddenly and for no reason adopting the voice of an escaped mental patient. "You know, this is what bunny rabbits like to eat! Say! let's pretend we're bunny rabbits!"

"No, I don't like this food! I don't like these people! I don't like this house! I wanna go home and eat hot dogs!"

As a last resort, I would employ my oldest and most consistently effective threat: "If you don't eat your dinner, you won't get any dessert!" Then I'd turn to the hosts and ask, with pleading eyes, "Uh, we *are* having dessert, aren't we?"

"Oh, yes," they'd respond. "We sure hope the little tyke likes rhubarb pie!"

The odds of salvaging any portion of the evening are now equal to Pee-wee Herman's shot at the papacy. Still, I would keep trying until the gala gathering wound down, and I'd suggest to my son that farewell handshakes were in order.

"NO!"

Well, then, could you at least say thank you for the very nice dinner?

"NO!"

How about good-bye?

"NO!"

On the way home, there is some solace in knowing you'll never have to relive the evening's scenario. Once word gets out, your popularity as party guests will rival that of convicted skunk molesters.

Your pride and joy, of course, will be oblivious to the sudden, ninety-degree plummet of his family's social status. "That was a fun party," he will say brightly, from the back seat. "Can we go back there tomorrow night?"

Pampered Lifestyles

The experts agree that mothers do not have a biological, psychological, or natural advantage that automatically makes them better kiddie-caretakers than fathers. Clearly, the experts have never watched a man change a diaper.

There are many areas in which dads excel. They grow superior mustaches. They can wear boxer shorts without looking ridiculous. And male is almost always the gender of choice when you need help push-starting a loaded pickup truck.

But none of these talents are so awe-inspiring as the average mother's ability to freshen up her baby as she flags down a bus. While running. And putting the finishing touches on her tax return.

Men will never master this task. But with the assistance of a seasoned father like myself, they *can* get through the ordeal without looking like helpless boobs.

How to Change a Diaper in Less than Three Hours and Fifteen Minutes

1. Determine if the child *needs* his diaper changed. If you're lucky, there will be visible signs of leakage. If you're unlucky, those signs will be all over your trousers and shirt.

When the need for clean drawers does not announce itself, many mothers size up the situation by poking an index finger down the back of the diaper and feeling around. This, to me, seems a rather extreme method when a simple x-ray could supply you with an answer that's just as accurate and many times more sanitary.

If you've yet to work an x-ray machine into your nursery decor, it is still unneccesary to resort to investigation by index finger. Simply pinch the back of the diaper, pull it away, and make a visual check. If you can't bring yourself to look (no man on the planet would blame you), just inhale. This will tell you everything you need to know—although you may suddenly understand why the index-finger method is so popular.

2. With breath held and eyes closed to avoid any further sensory contact with whatever's in there, peel off the diaper tape. (You *are* using disposable diapers, aren't you? If not, give up. You're a madman and well beyond any help I could give you.) As you prop the baby's legs upward with one hand, reach for the premoistened baby wipes and remove one from the handy dispenser top. Go ahead, I'll wait.

Dum dee dee dum dum dum, dee dee dum dum dee . . .

61

3.   At this point, mothers usually apply lotion, cream, or powder to the baby. As far as I'm concerned, however, there's a far more important task at hand: getting rid of the used diaper. Sometimes you can merely toss it into the nearest wastebasket... but sometimes you must encase it in lead, drive to a remote, unpopulated area, and bury it at a depth of no less than fifteen feet.

4.   When the disposal is complete, open your eyes and resume breathing.

5.   Should you suddenly realize you're out of fresh diapers, don't panic. You may be mistaken. If it turns out you're *not* mistaken, panic.

Otherwise, slide the new diaper under the baby, tape-end up. With one hand, pull the bottom half up between the baby's legs and hold it against his stomach. With the other hand, locate the tape pull-tab on the left. And with your other hand, grope for the pull tab on the right.

6.   If you happen to have any leftover hands, wrap the diaper's upper left-rear corner around the baby's waist while keeping a firm, but not yet tab-pulling, grip on the pull-tab. When it's in place, pull the tab and use some idle limb or bodily protrusion (i.e., your nose) to adhere the tape to the diaper's upper left-front corner.

7.   As you continue to apply pressure to the tape so it won't pop open and refuse to stick to anything ever again, move to the right side and repeat step six and the first half of step seven. If all your body parts are busy, scream for help.

8.   Congratulations. You now have a freshly diapered baby—*and* you've proven that you're not a total washout as a father. Enjoy the sensation, because it won't last long. In fact, if your child didn't soil himself anew while you were changing his diaper, he is surely doing so now.

9.   Cancel any plans you might have had for the rest of the day, hold your breath, close your eyes, and repeat steps one through eight until the cows, or some women, come home.

Masked Marvels

This Halloween, my son is demanding to be outfitted like his favorite, two-bit Japanese creature-feature star, Ghidrah, the Three-Headed Monster, and his expectations are high.

I'm sure he thinks he'll be able to climb into the thing, fly off, barbecue cities with his multiple fire-breathing noggins, and stomp the sushi out of millions of Asian pedestrians as they run amok and scream "AIIIIIIII!"

I'm not about to dampen the boy's excitement by telling him that, at best, if he can locate the front porch through his eyeholes, he might be able to stomp a few crickets and *maybe* frighten some of the younger neighborhood kids—provided they don't get close enough to notice that two of his heads are actually green gym socks stuffed with toilet paper.

Pardon the digression, but I am reminded of a thought-provoking scene in my son's favorite motion picture, the all-star Japanese monster-epic *Destroy All Monsters!* As Godzilla wades toward Tokyo with an especially mischievous look in his eyes, the action cuts to a television reporter who warns his viewers, "Godzilla is in Tokyo harbor! Repeat! Godzilla is in Tokyo Harbor! This is not a drill!"

Does this mean Tokyo actually stages regular Godzilla drills? Pretty hard to imagine. Godzilla has trashed the place hundreds of times, yet its population is never prepared to do anything but run amok and scream "AIIIIIIII!"

Some are so stupid as to try to escape by train—and as any child in my house can tell you, the first thing a rampaging, ninety-ton, radioactive lizard is gonna do is pick up the train, peek in the windows, and practice his javelin toss. Doesn't anyone mention this during the Godzilla drills?

It's a mystery.

Anyway, back to my son's Ghidrah suit. I've been trying to talk him into simpler and more traditional Halloween regalia. When I was a boy, I was always a cowboy or a clown or a hobo. I never figured out why until I had my own kids. All it took for my mother to transform me into a clown was a couple of lipstick circles on my cheeks. For the cowboy motif, she'd hand me a dime-store Stetson and a squirt gun. The hobo disguise required no effort whatsoever; she'd just dress me in my regular clothes and send me outside to play. A few hours later —presto!—I looked like a hobo.

One Halloween I begged her to let me make my candy-mongering rounds as a ghost. She finally relented, but refused to cut eyeholes in a perfectly good sheet. I don't remember the outcome. I either went out as a blind ghost or an unmade bed, one or the other.

At least my mother didn't play favorites. My younger sister, Lisa, was always a princess, a ballerina, or a child prostitute. Of the latter outfit, I'm sure Mom had something else in mind, like a Mary Kay Cosmetics rep or something. But if my sister had cruised the neighborhood looking like that on any other night, we'd *all* have been arrested.

Today's kids are wise to these money- and effort-saving ploys. Oh, when they're one or two years old you can still dress them any way you want. But when they start to suspect you're not the all-giving, all-sacrificing parent you pretend to be, they want nothing to do with your lame, low-budget ideas.

No, the older they get, the more their primary aim is to slip into a costume that will induce heart attacks, strokes, or, at the very least, nausea.

It's a distressing trend, but more and more, today's youngsters get their costume inspiration from the most grotesque and repulsive characters in Hollywood. Last year, for example, my doorbell was rung by short, stomach-churning incarnations of Freddy Krueger *(A Nightmare on Elm Street)*, Jason Voorhees *(Friday the 13th)*, Leatherface *(The Texas Chainsaw Massacre)*, and Shelley Winters ("The New Super Password").

All things considered, I'm thrilled that my son wants to trick-or-treat as Ghidrah, the Three-Headed Monster. Given the choice, I'd rather have a kid who wants to squish and charbroil innocent pedestrians than rip them apart limb by limb and hack up their torsos with power tools. Just call me old-fashioned.

By the way, my son wants me to wear a costume, too. He's even promised to help me make it. I asked him how I should dress up, and he wasted no time coming up with an answer. "I know!" he exclaimed. "Why don't you be a big, fat, hairy guy!"

My mother would have been proud of him.

If you're otherwise occupied this Halloween, too bad. You're gonna miss the once-in-a-lifetime sight of Ghidrah, the Three-Headed Monster fireballing our neighborhood, followed by a big, fat, hairy guy hollering, "This is not a drill! I repeat! This is not a drill!"

AIIIIIIII!

Touchy Topic

"Don't play with your genitals at the supper table!"

The evening my wife first glared at our four-year-old son and introduced this new entry in our household book of rules, she turned to me and added, "That goes for *you*, too."

Frankly, it's taken a lot of the fun out of our family meals. But it's made for a much more comfortable atmosphere when we have dinner guests.

Just kidding. It is, however, one of the more reliable facts of life that all boys will, at one time or another, make the innocent discovery that some body parts are more interesting than others. Another is that they are thrilled to note the difference.

But of the trillions of embarrassing habits a child can develop, public self-diddling is among the first that should be discouraged. I mean, think about it. There's not much that's quite so frightening as the thought that your kid will one day be awarded the Nobel Peace Prize, only to have your neighbors say, "You know, that was quite a stirring acceptance speech your son delivered on the national news last night. But I think it would have been much more effective if he hadn't had his hand down his pants."

See? You just can't let things like this slide.

Unfortunately, this is one of those areas where rules alone aren't always enough to modify behavior. Sometimes, the child will demand to know why the rules exist.

That process can be a snap when you're armed with cold, hard facts, such as, "Son, the reason you should never reach in the garbage disposal to retrieve your Ultra-Man poseable action figure is that your arm could get chewed off at the nub and you'll never learn to tie your own shoelaces."

But it's not so easy when you're dealing with some of society's more elusive right-and-wrong concepts while also trying to teach your child not to be ashamed of his body.

Tell such a kid to stop playing with his genitals at the supper table, and he will respond—as my son did—with the one word human beings utter more often than any other between their first spanking and their first apartment:

"Why?"

I wanted to answer, "Because. Now eat your dinner." But as a modern parent, I am deeply committed to maintaining the strong line of communication I like to think I've established with my son.

"Sweetheart, listen. Are you listening? Stop throwing your broccoli at the cat and *listen!* Are you listening? I said *stop that! Right now!* Okay. Now, the reason you shouldn't play with your genitals at the dinner table—or anywhere else, for that matter—is that it's not a nice thing to do."

"It's bad?"

"Yes. It's bad."

"Like killing?"

"No. It's not bad like that. It's . . . it's just not nice."

"No, Daddy. It's nice. You try it!"

"Honey, I don't mean that it doesn't *feel* nice . . . Uh, well, ahhh, I don't mean that it *does* feel nice, either. I mean, ummm, well, never mind. What I mean to say is that it isn't *polite.*"

"What's 'polite'?"

"You know how Mommy and Daddy always ask you to say 'please' and 'thank you' and 'excuse me' because it's *polite,* so everyone will think you're a nice boy?"

"Yeah."

"Well, they won't think you're a nice, polite boy if you sit at the supper table doing *that.* Do you understand?"

"Yes, Dad. If I do *this,* I should say 'excuse me.'"

"DON'T DO THAT!"

"Don't do what?"

"THAT!"

"It's bad?"

"YES! I mean, no but..."

"It's not polite?"

"That's right. By George, I think you've got it. It's not polite."

"WHY?"

We've been replaying this conversation nearly every night at the supper table for the past two weeks. I'll keep you posted on how it turns out. But in the future, if you ever turn on the evening news and see someone accepting a Nobel Peace Prize with his hands down his pants, don't blame his parents.

Vow Wows

I started out as a model parent. And I'd still be a model parent if my wife had had a hysterical pregnancy instead of a kid.

Before my son was born, the rules by which he'd live his life were all chartered out. I'd witnessed the mistakes of other mothers and fathers, and was not about to repeat them. I'd seen children play their daddies like a Mister Music piano, and vowed that no kid would ever get the upper hand on MY keys.

Among veteran procreators, that last sentence is one of millions sniggeringly referred to as Famous Last Words.

There aren't many ultimate truths in this world, but here's one of them: Nothing—repeat, *nothing*—is easier than looking at someone else's offspring and noting where their parents are going horribly wrong. But once you're face-to-cherubic-face with your own precious heirs, it's damned near impossible to put what you've learned into practice.

For the benefit of model-parents-in-waiting, I offer some of the more infamous Famous Last Words . . . and the clauses you'll be adding to them in no time flat.

"I will not let my my child watch that cheap, violent, mind-warping kiddie-crap they show on Saturday morning television . . ."

Clause: " . . . unless I'm busy, want to sleep in, or just don't feel like dealing with the screams."

70

"I will never spank my child in public, especially while in line at the supermarket..."

Clause: "...except when verbal threats of violence fail to attract his attention, or when the brat is really, truly asking for it."

"My child will get no dessert until he's cleaned his plate..."

Clause: "...or the dog has cleaned his plate. Or I have cleaned his plate. Or *somebody* has cleaned his plate. Or he loses his plate."

"I will give my child candy only as a rare and special reward for outstanding behavior..."

Clause: "...like when he stops crying, begging, and groveling for the stuff long enough for me to open the wrapper."

"I will not tolerate any rude noises in public..."

Clause: "...unless the public finds his rude noises amusing. On those occasions, rude noises will be encouraged."

"I absolutely, positively will not tolerate whining..."
Clause: "...and as soon as I can think of an effective way to keep him from whining, it *will* stop!"

"I will never attempt to buy my child's affection with gifts..."
Clause: "...unless the gifts are relatively inexpensive and I'm in need of a little extra affection."

"I will always remember what it's like to be a kid..."
Clause: "...except when I'm consumed with what it's like being an adult."

"I will not spoil my child..."
Clause: "...until he has emerged from the birth canal, at which time spoiling him will become my hobby and reason to live."

"I will never attempt to manipulate my kid with threats I have no intention of carrying out..."
Clause: "...unless the threats I *do* intend to carry out have no effect whatsoever."

"I will never put my child to bed without first giving him a goodnight kiss..."

So far, those are the only Famous Last Words I haven't been forced to eat. But according to my wife, I'm a model parent, anyway. "And you know what a model is," she likes to explain. "It's a small, cheap imitation of the real thing."

Cold War

I do not handle illness well. Give me a mild case of the sniffles or up my body temperature to 98.7 and I immediately slip into my impersonation of Ali McGraw in *Love Story*. I shuffle around the house, moaning softly and reminding my wife that love means never having to say you're sorry.

Eventually, she'll beg me to suffer in silence—at which point I will apologize (in real life, love means having to say you're sorry three or four hundred times a day), return to my deathbed, and amend my will.

Nowadays, I'm sniffling, shuffling, and apologizing more than ever before. You see, living with a preschooler is like owning your very own Germ and Virus Home Delivery Service.

For some reason, young'uns are the carrier of choice among microscopic vermin, perhaps because they're close to the ground and easier to board. Whatever the explanation, as soon as a new cold or flu bug hits town, the first place it heads is the nearest preschool, and the first greenish goo it generates will flow from the nose of your bundle of joy.

Soon the child will be hacking and sneezing and trying to survive a fever that could thaw a frozen turkey from ten feet. He will show no sign of recovery until the symptoms are passed to one family member, then another, then another.

Weeks later, when your clan at last seems on the verge of renewed good health, the whole, horrid cycle begins again. This scenario will continue until your child 1) runs away from home, 2) goes off to college, 3) elopes, 4) is sold to medical science, or 5) is adopted out to some healthy, childless, unsuspecting couple who will be eternally grateful until they realize they're spending $37,000 per year on Vitamin C alone.

Fortunately, my son is no chip off the sniveling block. This kid isn't about to let a few overactive snot glands turn *him* into a pathetic shell of a human being like his old man. He can be flirting with double pneumonia, and he'll *still* beg to go outside and roughhouse with his pals. The only thing that will slow him down is any casual use of the word "doctor," which inspires the lad to improvise a soliloquy reminiscent of the scene in *Rain Man* where the Dustin Hoffman character expresses his opinion of air travel.

My son's only other weakness in this area is that he was born with a hair-trigger gag reflex and just about anything can set it off. He's been known to toss his Gummi Bears at the sight of Grandma's cat walking in the general direction of its litter box. And when he's *really* sick, the little darling consistenty breaks his own records in the areas of quantity, force, distance, and poor marksmanship.

But he doesn't whimper or whine; he just upchucks and gets on with his life. This isn't a trait I brag about when showing off wallet-sized snapshots of the boy, yet I'll wager that even Arnold Schwarzenegger can't spend an entire day porcelain-bowlside without emitting at least one between-heave groan.

Last week my son was as sick as he's ever been, and he handled it with typical bravery. I'd just finished reading him Dr. Seuss's *Green Eggs and Ham* (which, incidentally, is *not* the ideal bedtime story for a sick child with a hair-trigger gag reflex) when he asked, without a trace of fear, "Dad, am I gonna die?"

"Of course, not, sweetheart."

"But when my goldfish got sick, he died. Now I'm sick, so I'm gonna die, too. Right?"

"Honey, you're just a *little* sick. You're going to get better."

MICHAEL BURKETT

Long pause.

"Dad, I'm waiting, but I'm still not better. I think I'm gonna die."

"Sweetie, believe me, you aren't going to die."

"But if I do . . . are there toys in heaven?"

I'm pleased to report that my son has recovered and no longer frets about spending the rest of eternity dead and toyless. The only reason I'm not overcome with joy is that, obviously, it's time to start stocking up on Kleenex and practicing my Ali McGraw impression.

74

'Night Father

Bedtime for Bonzo, Jr. II: The Saga Continues

Another Compelling True-Life
Sci-Fi Docudrama in One Act

(As the curtain rises, the large, bearded man is tucking the small, unbearded boy into bed.)

BOY: Daddy, will you read me a story?

MAN: Sure, son.

BOY: How about *Benji the Hunted?*

MAN: That's not a book, sweetheart. It's a movie. We saw it a long time ago. I don't think I remember the story.

BOY: Please, Daddy! Tell me *Benji the Hunted.*

MAN: Well, okay. I'll try, Ummm, let's see. One day, Benji was lost in the woods, far away from home . . .

BOY: What about the boat?

MAN: What boat?

BOY: The boat that turned over in the ocean and Benji had to swim to land.

MAN: Oh, yeah. One day, Benji was on a boat that turned over in the ocean and he had to swim to land. And there he was, lost in the woods, far away from home . . .

BOY: Don't forget the helicopter.

MAN: Helicopter?

BOY: The helicopter that's looking for Benji, to save him.

MAN: Oh, right. I was just getting to that part. When Benji was lost in the woods, he looked up and saw helicopters!

BOY: Just one helicopter, Dad.

MAN: Who's telling this story, anyway?

BOY: You.

MAN: I'm glad we finally got *that* settled. Soooo, Benji looked up and saw a helicopter, but it flew away. Then he saw a big, mean wolf!

BOY: The wolf comes later. After Benji finds the baby cougars.

MAN: Okay, son. You tell *me* the story.

BOY: No! No! Please, Daddy! You tell it. Please?

MAN: All right. But no more interruptions, okay? Now where were we?

BOY: The wolf came before Benji found the baby cougars and he wasn't supposed to.

MAN (long pause): Riiiight. When the helicopter flew away, Benji found some baby cougars ...

BOY: Daddy?

MAN: *What?!?*

BOY: You forgot about the baby cougars' mommy.

MAN: What *about* the baby cougars' mommy?

BOY: She gets shot by a hunter. That's why Benji has to take care of the baby cougars ... (looong pause) ... Daddy? ... Are you going to tell me the rest of the story, Daddy? ... Daddy?

MAN: No, I am *not* going to tell you the rest of the story unless you promise to be quiet! Are you going to be quiet? Otherwise, it's lights out! And I mean it!

BOY: I'll be quiet.

MAN: You'd better. I'm not kidding. This is your last chance. Now, let's see ...

BOY: The helicopter flew away.

MAN: Right. The helicopter flew away, and Benji saw a hunter shoot the mommy cougar. That's when he found the baby cougars.

BOY: (whispering): Daddy?

MAN: That's it. The light is going off. Good night, son. (Turns off light, exits.)

BOY: No, Daddy! I just needed to ask you somethin'!

MAN VOICE: Sorry. You promised to be quiet. Good night.

BOY (crying): Daddy? Will . . . will . . . will Jesus take care of the mommy cougar?

MAN: Wonderful. (Enters, turns on light.) Yes, honey. Jesus will take care of the mommy cougar.

BOY (instantly cheered): Then what happens?

MAN: Benji leads the baby cougars through the forest, and they see the big, mean wolf!

BOY (softly): A mean man.

MAN: What?

BOY: A mean man ties Benji up. But Benji gets away, and *then* they see the big, mean wolf. He chases Benji and falls off a big cliff and goes "Owwwwwwwwwwwwwwwwww!" And he's dead!

MAN: What happens next?

BOY: I don't know, Daddy. *You're* telling the story.

MAN: I'll tell you what happens next. They all go to Benji's house and live happily ever after. The end. Good night. (Turns off light, starts to exit.)

BOY: Daddy? Will you tell me that story again tomorrow night?

MAN: Only if I'm stricken by temporary insanity.

(Blackout. Curtain. Scream.)

Birthday Bash

I used to look forward to my son's birthday, but the event isn't nearly as much fun as it once was. The boy has caught on.

First birthdays are the best. One-year-olds have no idea what a birthday is, and no expectations mean no disappointments. You don't have to deck the walls with balloons and crepe-paper streamers. You aren't required to let a mob of unruly party guests drool ice cream, cake frosting, and assorted kid-juices all over your house. Nor must you chaperone them to one of those numbingly cute theme-pizzerias for the ugliest afternoon of your life.

Heck, when you get right down to it, you don't even have to shell out for birthday presents, because your yearling doesn't know what *those* are, either.

Should you feel compelled to observe the tradition, however, you can buy the kid a vacuum cleaner, a VCR, or a new refrigerator; slap some brightly colored ribbons on it; sing a few lively choruses of "Happy Birthday"; and go to bed confident that, by morning, Junior will have no memory whatsoever of his lavish "gift," the gala bash thrown in his honor, or *you*, for that matter.

Not only that, you'll be the proud owner of a brand-new household appliance you never would have purchased for yourself.

Second birthdays are almost as nice. At that age, kids are just beginning to get the idea that there's *something* special about the occasion, but the concept of automatic gift-getting continues to elude them.

And since most two-year-olds have yet to master the art of counting, one fabulous gift is just as exciting as a thousand. Even better, paper-bag puppets qualify as fabulous gifts.

If the birthday babe has developed an early knack for numbers, you can still save big dough by creating the optical illusion that he's being showered with treasures. It's easy. Just hand the child a paper-bag puppet, distract him ("Look! A squirrel!" works every time), snatch the puppet away, regain his attention, and give it to him again. After a few hours of this, any two year-old in the world would consider you generous to a fault.

Regrettably, such deceptions don't work as well by the time year three rolls around. Thanks to his blabbermouth pals, the little man is now hip to the benefits to be wrung from this, his own, personal holiday. He knows how to count, he's aware that birthdays mean *more stuff,* and he expects the guest list to include every kid he ever met —not only to guarantee a heavy payload of gifts, but also to show them all the neat, new plastic junk he owns and *they don't.*

Although these discoveries take a good deal of fun out of the proceedings, parents continue to have an advantage because even the sharpest three-year-olds aren't *real* bright. It's tricky, but if you make a huge fuss over whatever horribly lame or practical gift it is you're trying to palm off on them, most youngsters of this age can be convinced they've struck the mother lode.

"WOW! Look what you got! I don't believe it! A WHOLE BAG OF SOCKS! Ooooooh, you're so LUCKY. You must be a VERY SPECIAL BOY to get A WHOLE BAG OF SOCKS for your birthday! GOSH, do you think I could BORROW a pair of those WONDERFUL SOCKS one day?"

Don't worry about overdoing it. You can't. It will be another five or six months before your offspring begins to suspect that you're untrustworthy, and at least one year before he's absolutely certain of it.

My son is about to celebrate his fifth birthday, and he's approaching the big day like a seasoned pro. Now a full-fledged material boy, he knows there will be a big party and that he'll bag several tons of merchandise whether he's good, naughty, or suddenly gets the urge to become a serial killer.

He can spot grown-up excitement faster than he can locate the toy section in a department store.

He's fully prepared to make Mommy and Daddy's life miserable if they don't deliver exactly what he's ordered.

And anyone who shows up at the festivities with a vacuum cleaner, a paper-bag puppet, or a bag of socks is begging to be struck from the "God bless" list at the end of his nightly prayers.

Ah, well. He's my son, it's his birthday, and I wouldn't dream of cheating him out of it. Not until he starts demanding to celebrate at a theme-pizzeria, anyway.

Rocky's Hurt

Sometimes, as that popular bumper sticker so ineloquently puts it, shit happens. And sometimes, there is no one to blame.

You can see it coming from fifty miles off, all flashing lights and screaming sirens. You can do everything in your power to avoid it. And then... shit happens. Like it's never happened before. Not in your life, anyway.

Rocky Graham had a hurt that his mommy and daddy and the doctor couldn't take away.

Rocky was a handsome, basketball-addicted sixteen-year-old kid who seemed exceptionally bright despite his uncanny knack for making bad decisions.

Really bad decisions.

I didn't know him well, and it always seemed like he wanted to keep it that way. Whenever we saw each other, the most I'd get out of him was a distracted "Hi." Only once did we exchange enough words to qualify as a conversation.

We'd been at the same pool party the night before, a gathering of families. Rocky, the son of two close friends, had brought along a pal. As usual, they kept their distance from the crowd. While everyone else swam and ate and laughed, they remained in the house, as quiet as kids who don't exist. So when I returned to the room where I'd left my clothes—and found my wallet on the floor, open and emptier than I'd left it—there wasn't an overwhelming number of suspects to choose from.

Mentioning the theft to Rocky's folks was one of the most difficult things I've ever done. After all, most mothers and fathers don't take too kindly to anyone, friends included, accusing their children of stealing. But Rocky's parents had no illusions about their son. Flushed with rage and embarrassment, they stormed into the house, and soon returned with the missing money.

My friends went home a short while later, still angry to the point of speechlessness. And Rocky? "See ya," he shrugged, as if nothing had happened.

But the next day, Rocky called to apologize. Perhaps his parents were looming over him at the time, and that's why he sounded so horribly uncomfortable. I prefer to think he was suffering the pangs of remorse. Very often, the best you could give this kid was the benefit of the doubt.

That was a year and a half ago. Unfortunately, Rocky did not transform into a model teenager. He moved from hanging out with the wrong crowd to joining the wrong crowd. From skipping class to dropping out of school. From vanishing now and then to vanishing, period. From stealing petty cash from friends to stealing a stranger's car . . . and finally, to stealing from himself.

There are a number of self-proclaimed experts who could very neatly explain how Rocky's mind worked, why it worked that way, and what should have been done to tighten up its most dangerously loose connections. But I doubt that they'd come up with any theories left unconsidered or untested by Rocky's parents. Tough love, soft love, professional help, spiritual guidance, friendly advice, public school, private school—they tried it all. And while their patience was known to fray, it never unraveled.

Last month, Rocky's father and I spent the better part of an afternoon talking about the boy—who'd just run away from home because his parents were so cruel as to expect him to attend high school on a regular basis.

"Maybe what he needs is a taste of reality," said Rocky's dad.

"Maybe he needs to take one long, hard fall when there's nobody around to catch him. Maybe that will get his attention. I pray to God it does, because I honestly don't know what else we can do for him. Hell, we don't even know where he is.

"If only we could get him to realize how lucky he is to have so many people who love him, who believe in him, who want the best for him. If only we could know that he's gonna be okay, and that one day the whole family will be able to sit back and laugh about all the crap he put us through when he was a kid."

That last, small hope was shattered last week, when Rocky Graham made the worst decision of his life. He was found dead, a bullet in his brain, a gun near his hand, an apparent suicide.

His parents had done everything they could. But, as they explained to their son's four-year-old sister, Rocky had a hurt that his mommy and daddy and doctor couldn't take away.

Sometimes, shit happens. And there is no one to blame.

The Time Machine

This morning, my son told me that he and his pal Brian are going to build a time machine so they can zap themselves back to prehistory and cavort with the dinosaurs. Should they succeed, I'm going to ask him to drop me off in my own childhood. Nothing against the Jurassic period, but it hardly seems as exciting as a world where anything is possible.

It is said that we start dying the minute we're born. Well, you needn't look any further than two kids building a time machine to know it's true. It's not just the ability to fantasize such an adventure that we lose at a horribly early age; other losses include a child's absolute faith in himself and his absolute certainty that everything is going to turn out just as he's dreamed it.

Sure, there are disadvantages to being a kid. There is homework, household chores, visits to the doctor, siblings with no sense of territorial imperative, the constant demand to behave as if they were older, wiser, quieter, or, in short, someone else.

On top of that, there are all those pesky rules: No, you can't bomb your baby sister with G.I. Joe hand grenades ... no, you can't get out the ladder so you and the neighbor kids can play "King of the Roof" ... no, you can't eat leftover Halloween candy for breakfast.

On the whole, though, kids are pretty lucky. They can find a penny on the sidewalk and feel as rich as Scrooge McDuck. They can find a fossil-shaped rock and feel like Indiana Jones. They can find an anthill and feel like God.

Kids never feel guilty for eating too much or exercising too little or squandering their money on things they don't really need. They can run buck naked through the sprinkler without giving a millisecond's thought to what the neighbors might think of their chubby thighs, imperfect waistlines, or moral standards.

When kids are sick, everything in the world comes to a stop except Mom, the Campbell Soup Co., and daytime TV.

When they get mail, it's always good news: a letter from a friend, a magazine, a greeting card, a long-awaited box-top prize. They only get telephone calls from people they're happy to talk to. And their visitors rarely have any greater aim than to find a playmate or show off a new toy.

Kids can throw their dirty clothes on the floor, confident in the magical forces that will somehow return them, clean and folded, to their dresser drawers. These are much the same benevolent forces which provide most kids at birth with food, toys, money, and a houseful of people who love them.

Kids don't have to carry wallets, purses, keys, makeup, combs, identification, or cash. They don't have to wait in line at the bank, or wait in line at the supermarket, or wait in line for anything but good stuff like movies and dodge ball and Happy Meals, where waiting in line is part of the thrill.

It's easy to disappoint a kid, but not for long. The pain of canceled plans and rainy days quickly gives way to the joys of free time, imagination, and long-forgotten treasures that sifted to the bottom of the toy box.

Kids are so wonderfully unsophisticated they're incapable of judging people by how they look, what they do for a living, or how smart or successful they are. Their sole precondition for friendship is friendliness. And if you get down on the floor with them for a few minutes, you'll have a blood brother for life.

To a kid, there are no unanswered questions. What they can't figure out for themselves, Mom and Dad can explain. And when Mom and

Dad are stumped, there's always Grandpa, who watches "Jeopardy!" and therefore knows everything.

Kids never fail to see the wonder in shooting stars and the man in the moon. Yet nothing is quite so awe-inspiring as the sight of a frog hopping around right on their own patio.

When adults cry, it is usually for themselves, over lives that somehow didn't turn out as expected. Kids cry for themselves, too—but only briefly, over mere moments that have gone wrong. Their deepest, most sorrowful tears are reserved for genuine disasters, like the discovery of a baby bird that never got the chance to fly.

Even so, kids believe that death means falling down, getting back up, and resuming play. It's not something that actually happens to people. To kids, life is forever.

And in a sense, they're right. When you live and play and cry and love entirely for the moment, as kids do, there's no such thing as time. Only time machines.

Nothing But the Tooth

It's a paradox. You try to instill in your child a deep, abiding respect for truth and honesty. You strive to establish a firm base of mutual trust. Yet you can look the kid straight in the eye and tell him that when his teeth fall out, he should put them under his pillow so a winged denizen of brownieland can sneak into his room at night, swap his baby bicuspids for cash, then vanish into the darkness like a deranged ivory poacher.

If you're lucky, your little innocents will blindly accept the tooth-fairy story, much as they accept Santa Claus, the Easter Bunny, and (in some households) Lothar the Brat-Eating Cyclops.

But if you're unlucky, like me, the kid will scream, "I don't want no strange lady comin' in my room while I'm sleepin'!"

"She's not a strange lady," I explained to my newly gap-toothed boy. "She's a pixie. Like, ahhhh ... Tinkerbell. Yeah! Like Tinkerbell."

"Dad, Tinkerbell's a *cartoon.* She's not real."

It's a sad tale, indeed, when a five-year-old has a stronger grasp on reality than his father. My only recourse at this point was to utterly confuse the boy.

"No, no," I said. "I don't mean Tinkerbell in the Disney movie. I mean Tinkerbell in that other *Peter Pan* tape you watch."

"You mean where Peter Pan is a lady?"

"Ummm, yeah," I grumbled, wondering how it was possible for such a bright child to emerge from my gene pool.

I was certain I'd lost the lad completely until he shrugged and said,

"Okay, The tooth fairy is like the *real* Tinkerbell. So what does she want with my teeth?"

I called my wife into the room. She always knows the answers to these kinds of questions. And frankly, I couldn't wait to hear the explanation myself.

According to her, and I quote, "The tooth fairy takes your teeth and gives them to new babies who don't have any."

That line of reasoning pleased my son, but it revolted the heck out of me. Life seems hard enough without starting off at square one with a mouth full of used teeth. And what about that popular parental warning, "Don't put that in your mouth! You don't know where it's been!" If you don't know where your *teeth* have been, what's the point?

Alas, there was no time to solve that riddle, because my son needed help with a few mental puzzles of his own—such as, "How will the tooth fairy get under my pillow if my head is on it?"

Believe it or not, I knew the answer to that one: "It's magic!" Even the smartest kids believe in magic. Without it, there'd be no babies in the world, birds couldn't fly, and parents would go stark-raving wacky trying to explain elusive concepts to their children.

"How much money will I get?" my son asked, getting down to the nitty-gritty.

"Well, how much do you think you should get?"

"Two thousand dollars," he estimated. Obviously, we are raising a born dentist. Who else would equate one tooth with the down payment on a new car?

As soon as the boy ran out of questions (a first, I think), a private father-mother conference was held to determine how much a child's tooth might actually be worth in today's tooth-fairy market.

"A quarter," my wife stated with absolute confidence.

"A *quarter?*" I parried. "Let's give him fifty cents, at least. You can't buy anything for a quarter nowadays."

"You can't buy anything for fifty cents, either."

She had me there. Still, a quarter seems awfully cheap for a body part. Especially one that belongs to your own child, and that prompted excited phone calls all over the country when it sprouted out of his head.

But I relented, taking comfort in the fact that, by morning, I could stop lying to my son for the first time since his tooth started wobbling two weeks ago. And he could stop suspecting that his father is a big, fat liar.

What I'd failed to take into account is that children are greedy little capitalists who will do anything for money, candy, or toys, provided it doesn't require effort, an attention span, or the consumption of green, leafy vegetables. As soon as my son had his first tooth-fairy cash in hand, he started yanking on the rest of his teeth. By that afternoon, he'd pulled out another.

Clearly, whoever it was that started the Great American Tooth Fairy Lie is a cruel practical jokester, and I am his patsy. By this time next month, I'll have a son who looks like Gabby Hayes, Jr., and nary a quarter to my name.

And Baby Makes Four

All babies fall into two categories: the kind you try and try and try to produce, and the kind that seem to produce themselves when your mind is on something else.

Our boy was Type One. In this week's episode, we introduce Type Two.

Now, call me silly, but the main reason I've been mulling over the purchase of one of those Black & Decker Home Vasectomy Kits is that I can't imagine loving another kid as much as I love my son.

Intellectually, I realize that parental affection isn't like the fruit in a grade-school arithmetic problem, where if you have three apples and give one apiece to Johnny, Mary, and Moonbeam, you're plum outta apples. But emotionally, the last thing I want is to bring a new child into this touch-and-go world and *then* discover I'm short a few Granny Smiths.

My wife and I had been talking about doubling our parental pleasure, and I was happy to leave it at that. Talk, as they say, is cheap. And it's the bargain of the century when compared to the cost of bringing up babies.

So far, for me, one of the greatest thrills of fatherhood was hearing the victorious squeal, "Daddy! Look! I went in the potty!" Naturally, I was proud of my son—but I was *ecstactic* for myself. No longer would I have to sign my paychecks over to the disposable diaper division of Proctor & Gamble. We could start saving for things we'd always wanted, like a subscription to *TV Guide.* In time, who knew? Maybe we could get a TV, too.

It was another landmark day when my son stopped growing two inches an hour. Prior to that, whenever we bought him clothes, we'd have to race from the store, barrel home, and deck the kid in his new apparel before he outgrew it. If we hit one red light, we'd be stuck with $157-worth of brand-new hand-me-downs.

Bearing all this and a possible apple shortage in mind, perhaps you can understand why I wasn't overcome with joy when my wife announced that we'd soon be increasing our household census count.

Of course, I wasn't about to ADMIT my reservations. If there's one thing I've learned after six years of marriage, it is that honesty is always the best policy ... except when your wife says something like "I'm pregnant!" and your most honest response is to run about the house screaming, "WHAT? WE CAN'T AFFORD ANOTHER KID! WE'LL HAVE TO MOVE IN WITH YOUR PARENTS UNTIL WE CAN SCRAPE TOGETHER ENOUGH MONEY TO LIVE IN OUR CAR! ARE YOU OUTTA YOUR SKULL?!?!?!?"

That level of candor can lead to a lengthy hospitalization and the permanent nickname "Gimpy."

Besides, the deed was done. It wasn't as if my wife had surprised me with a new $190 dress that would threaten our marital bliss only until it was returned to the store. Babies are nonrefundable. My only recourse was to shut up and get happy. Fast.

And I did. Thanks to my son.

He's been telling everyone he meets that Mommy's going to have a baby. He makes formal announcements in restaurants and supermarkets. He stops people on the street and invites them to feel his mother's tummy.

Every morning, he comes into our bedroom with a glass of water for the baby. When Mom is greenish from morning sickness, he worries that the baby might be suffering, too. So he covers my wife with his favorite blanket—the one that always makes HIM feel better.

He promises to teach his new brother or sister everything there is to know about dinosaurs. And hardly a waking hour passes when he fails to remind us how much he loves the baby, sight unseen.

MICHAEL BURKETT   Yeah, I know the two of them will be beating the Pop-Tarts out of each other in no time flat. But somehow, the thought of bringing another child into this particular world has started to sound pretty darned terrific. If we run out of money, heck, we can always move in with my wife's parents.

And if I run out of apples, I can just borrow a bushel or two from my son.

Bonzo Redux

Bedtime for Bonzo, Jr. III

Yet Another Compelling True-Life
Sci-Fi Docudrama in One Act
Overheard from the Next Room

(The curtain rises on the spectacularly messy bedroom of a four-year-old boy, who is being tucked into bed by his spectacularly pregnant mother.)

BOY: Mom, will you read me a story?

MOTHER: Yes. But just one. A short one. You have to get a good night's sleep tonight. Do you remember where you're going tomorrow?

BOY: Yeah! To see Aunt Cheryl's new baby.

MOTHER: That's right.

BOY: Mom, where do babies live before they're born?

MOTHER: You know. In their mother's tummies. Just like our new baby.

BOY: I mean before that.

MOTHER: Oh. Well, they, um ... before that, they're angels. Waiting for just the right time to come to earth to be with their mommies and daddies.

BOY: They're *angels?*

MOTHER: Uh-huh.

BOY: In *heaven?* With God and Jesus and my goldfish and all the other angels?

MOTHER: Er, well, yes.

BOY: So they *DIED?*

MOTHER: No, no, no...they just, um...which book did you want me to read? How about *Three Billy Goats Gruff?*

BOY: How did they get to heaven if they didn't die? I thought you had to die to get to heaven.

MOTHER: No, you don't have to die. You see, ahh...we all come from heaven. That's where God makes us. And then we, um, wait for our turn to come to Earth. (Clears throat.) *Three Billy Goats Gruff.* Once upon a time there were three...

BOY: When the baby comes to Earth, how does it get into the mommy's tummy?

MOTHER: Well, mommies have these little tiny eggs inside them...

BOY (excited): YOU MEAN YOU'RE GONNA LAY AN EGG?

MOTHER: No, I'm not going to lay an egg. You see, mommies have these little eggs inside them and, um, daddies have something inside of them, and when you, ahh, put it all together, the egg turns into a baby.

BOY: Really?

MOTHER: Yes. That's how you make babies.

(Long pause.)

BOY: I'd rather make candy.

MOTHER: I don't blame you. Okay. *The Three Billy Goats Gruff.* Once upon a...

BOY: So God *doesn't* make the baby.

MOTHER: Yes, He does. He just needs the Mommy and Daddy to help Him. Now, c'mon. It's getting late. If you want me to read you this story...

BOY: Does the egg hatch inside of your tummy?

MOTHER: Well, sort of, yes.

BOY: When our baby is born, can I keep the egg shells?

MOTHER: Oh, honey, there aren't any egg shells. It's all very compli-cated. You'll understand when you're bigger. I promise. All right? Let's read the story.

BOY: How does the baby come out of your tummy?

MOTHER: Well, do you remember that video we rented about the cat and the dog who were best friends?

BOY: Yes.

MOTHER: And do you remember the part where we saw the puppies being born?

BOY (shocked): You mean when they came out like poop?

MOTHER: Uh . . .

BOY: Our baby isn't going to come out like *that,* is it?

MOTHER: Well, ahh . . .

BOY: Oh, *gross!!!* I don't want to be there. I don't want to see it. I'm gonna stay with Grandma. Gro-ooo-osss. (Pause.) Mom? Where are you going? Aren't you going to read me *The Three Billy Goats Gruff?*

MOTHER: No. It's very late, and I think you've had enough stories for one night. Good night, sweetheart. (She exits.)

BOY: Mom? I didn't come out like that, did I? Mom? Mom? (Pause.) Oh, gross! I should have let her read *Three Billy Goats Gruff.* (Blackout. Curtain.)

Snow Job

It doesn't bother me that my brother-in-law calls me Mr. Potato Head. Nor do I mind that no one ever leaps to my defense. What's annoying is that, the older I get, the less defense there is to leap to.

To illustrate, imagine a typical family outing. Let's say Mr. and Mrs. Jones decide, as my wife and I did, to treat their desert-dwelling child to a day in the snow. The scenario would unfold thusly: The Joneses would drive to the mountains, have a jolly time, and return home. Chances are, their happy little trip would not evolve into . . . A WILDERNESS ORDEAL.

To my credit, I got my family to the mountains without a hitch. But I had no intention of stopping at some overcrowded spot where we'd be dodging stray snowballs and runaway inner tubes all afternoon. I wanted to give my kid the experience of frolicking in a pristine, untrampled blanket of fairy flakes.

Deep in the Godforsaken Middle of Nowhere, we came upon a narrow, snow-covered road leading off the highway, through an open gate, toward a veritable winter wonderland.

"That's it!" I declared.

"You're not going to try *driving* in there, are you?" my wife asked —and she had a point. We were traveling in a Ford Aerostar minivan with rear-wheel drive and four balding tires. The only off-road surfaces this baby's designed to handle are driveways and parking lots.

"Aw," I said, pulling off the highway, "the worst that could happen is we'll get stuck and have to wait until spring to drive home."

Okay. Let's recap what's just happened. I sized up a situation, con-

cluded it was insane, and drove my family right into it. About a
hundred yards into it. Just far enough to discover that tires spinning
in snow actually *burn*, much like they do on pavement. Amazing.

"WE'RE STUCK HERE FOREVER, AREN'T WE?" my kid wailed
even before the smoke cleared.

"No we're not, honey," his mother cooed, so as not to frighten the
boy.

"WHATAWE GONNA DO? HOW'RE WE GONNA GET OUTTA
HERE?!?!"

"Calm down," my wife said gently. "You're scaring your son."

Her tone worried me. This is not a woman who handles ordeals
well. Especially wilderness ordeals. When she gets more than fifty
feet from an electrical outlet, she panics. I figured the stress had
pushed her over the edge. That meant our survival was up to me.

"Mom, what are we gonna do?" my son asked, trying to be brave.

"Oh, someone will come along and pull us out," she replied.

Hoo, boy. My wife was worse off than I'd thought. She could no
longer differentiate between a *wish* and a *plan*. And with a wish like
that, we could wind up like the Donner party, whose snowbound
members waited so long for help they ran out of food and ate each
other.

I thought back to all the true-life survival tales I'd read in *Reader's
Digest*. What was the first thing those people did when they found
themselves in a stare-down with death?

It came to me in a flash. They start a diary!

SUNDAY, 1:43 P.M.—We've been stranded for almost seven minutes. What to do? I get out of the car and check the tires. Yep. They're
stuck in the snow, all right. I get back into the car.

SUNDAY, 1:45 P.M.—Our sandwich supply is getting low. How long
can life be sustained on snow and tree bark? Not long, I think. My son
starts looking pretty darned tasty.

SUNDAY, 1:48 P.M.—My wife, still delirious, continues to believe
help will soon arrive. It's time for action. I recheck the tires.

SUNDAY, 1:51 P.M.—I have a plan! Since my wife can't drive a stick shift, I suggest she get out and push while I steer. She refuses on the grounds that she's eight months pregnant. My son refuses on the grounds that he's only five. I begin work on Alternate Plan B.

SUNDAY, 1:57 P.M.—My wife is reading. My son is napping. Obviously, they've given up hope. I'm still working on Alternate Plan B.

SUNDAY, 2:02 P.M.—A nice man with a large pickup truck tows us back to the main road. He then takes me aside and asks why I thought I could drive a Ford Aerostar minivan in two feet of snow. I tell him I was asleep in the back seat and my wife was driving.

SUNDAY, 2:08 P.M.—My son now thinks snow is evil and wants nothing more to do with the stuff.

SUNDAY, 5:14 P.M.—We arrive home. My brother-in-law drops by, hears my wife's version of the story, and calls me Mr. Potato Head. No one leaps to my defense. But the last laugh will be mine when I sell the book, movie, and *Reader's Digest* rights to my Wilderness Ordeal Diary.

I Kid You Not

If Bil "Family Circus" Keane can do it, so can I. I'm taking a vacation and turning this week's column over to my son. Ciao!

The Kid Zone

By Bonzo Burkett, Age 5

What's your favorite TV show? Mine is "Dink the Dinosaur." Do you like "Dink the Dinosaur"?

Okay. We can drop the act. Dad is loading his fishing poles into the car...he's pulling out of the driveway...he's gone. Now I can give you the real behind-the-scenes lowdown on this nutty new-baby hoax he's cooked up.

Oh, they had me fooled for a while there, too. About seven months ago, they sat me down and asked how I'd like a little brother or sister. I sez, "Compared to what?"

"No, really," they say. "We're gonna have a new baby in the family." And they're *smiling* when they make this announcement, like I'm supposed to think it's terrific news that I'll be losin' half my room, getting half as many toys for Christmas, and havin' to whine twice as loud to get any attention around here. Rejoice, rejoice.

"So, when does this new kid get here?" I ask.

"Not for a while yet."

Ever notice how hard it is to nail grown-ups down on *specifics?*

"Wead my wips," I say (they think it is sooo cute when I drop my r's and l's). "Gimme an *exact date.*"

"After Christmas."

That was hardly exact, but it was good news. At least I'd make one more merchandise haul before the competition showed up.

Anyway, Christmas comes, Christmas goes, still no baby. What's the deal here?

"We've still got a while to go."

That's the way it's been going for a couple of months now. Stall tactics and talk instead of *hard evidence.* And no, I haven't forgotten about the day Mom came home from the doctor with a "video sonogram."

"Bonzo!" she says. "How would you like to see a *movie* of our new baby?"

Oooooooh-kayyy, I'm thinking. Proof at last!

Mom slips the tape into the VCR...the picture comes up on the screen...and what do I see? Who knows?!?! It could be *anything.* My guess is that it's an out-of-focus black-and-white close-up of a washing machine during the rinse cycle.

"Look!" Mom exclaims. "There's the baby! There's your little brother or sister!"

Whoop-dee-doo. I'm gonna be sharing my room with a bouncing bundle of wet laundry. Break out the party hats and the noise-makers.

"See those two little black spots?" Mom asks, pointing at what looks to me like a pair of dirty socks. "Those are the baby's kidney's!"

Yeah. Sure. I can't even make out a *head* in this video Rorschach test, and she thinks she can see kidneys! This woman needs a vacation. Bad.

What I can't figure out is whether Mom actually believes what she's saying, or if she's been duped by some quack who takes home movies of his washing machine and peddles them to women who believe whatever cockamamie thing they're told.

I can just imagine the sales pitch: "And from this angle, Mrs. Burkett, you can see two tiny black areas. Those are...um...uhhh...

kidneys! Yeah! Kidneys! Now, will that be check, cash, or credit card?"

There's a sucker born every minute. But no matter what Dad tells you, none are scheduled for delivery in my house. We've already met our quota.

Special Delivery

If the *Guinness Book of World Records* ever adds categories for Speediest Birth and Shortest Radio Talk-Show Appearance, my wife and I will be international celebrities.

Shortly before scoring our dual triumphs, I was in a radio station newsroom preparing for a live, one-hour interview. My wife's due date was still three days away, but I called her anyway to find out if she'd gotten around to producing our second child.

"No, nothing's happening," she groaned. "Just these damned Braxton-Hicks contractions."

For the record, the term "Braxton-Hicks contractions" describes a cruel little practical joke Mother Nature likes to play on expectant mothers. If it's physical messages were translated into words, the gag would go something like this: "You're going to have the baby . . . You're going to have the baby . . . YOU'RE GOING TO HAVE THE BABY!!! . . . Ha ha ha, just kidding!"

Upon my bride's repeated assurances that she would remain a huge mother of one for at least another hour, I hung up and strolled into the studio. And if clouded memory serves, it was about four seconds after my live, on-air introduction that someone raced into the studio with a hurriedly scribbled sign that read, "Michael, your wife is in labor!"

Since the host of the show was named Michael, my first thought was to scream, "MICHAEL, YOUR WIFE IS IN LABOR!" But then I remembered that MY name is Michael, too, and that, more important,

I was the one with an incredibly pregnant wife suffering from "Braxton-Hicks contractions." Heh heh.

My next thought took me back to April 1, 1985, when we were awaiting the world debut of our son. My wife phoned me at work to announce that delivery was imminent and that I should meet her at the hospital as soon as possible. Not until I was numb with panic did she drop the ever-so-amusing punchline, "April Fools!"

Could this be *another* alleged "joke"? And if not, what now? Everyone knows that the old entertainment-world axiom "The Show Must Go On" applies to floods, earthquakes, and pestilence . . . but what about exploding wives?

Finally, I remembered that my wife was in labor twelve-and-a-half hours with our son. If she stuck to tradition, I could finish the show and still have eleven-and-a-half hours left over for a leisurely drive to the hospital. Maybe I could even take in a movie, grab a quick bite to eat, and shop for baby gifts along the way.

After some hemming and hawing from both of us, the host (who didn't know I was an expectant father and seemed to presume he was being filmed for an episode of "The New Candid Camera") said, "Uh, well, are you going to do something SCUMMY, like leave?" Clearly, it was his professional opinion that the show must go on, exploding wives or no.

Tough luck. I bid my adieu, flew out the door, and raced across town while wondering WHAT DAY IS THIS? IS THIS APRIL FIRST? THIS HAD BETTER NOT BE APRIL FIRST! IS THIS APRIL FIRST?

It wasn't.

My wife arrived at the hospital at 2:45 P.M., I got there at 2:48; and our perfect, fully inventoried baby daughter showed up around 2:53. Obviously, having experienced one twelve-and-a-half-hour labor, my wife chose not to do *that* again. Right there in the delivery room, without prior training, this woman had mastered the art of power-birthing.

And I had fathered the most beautiful baby girl in the world. That wasn't just my own biased and subjective opinion. Nary a nurse in the building could walk by this kid without gasping, "Why, that's the most beautiful baby girl in the world!"

These were total strangers who had no reason to lie. Not to me, at least. I'll admit that we heard them say the same thing to another brand-new dad whose baby looked like Ernest Borgnine *before* Mrs. Borgnine discovered that miracle facial cream. But what else could they say? "I thought your baby was wonderful on 'McHale's Navy'?"

Of course not.

It's a Miracle

They're not kidding when they call it "the miracle of birth." In addition to the obvious astonishments, it's a miracle that any woman who's experienced the agony once could ever suffer enough memory loss to say, "Yeah! I'd like to do that again!!!"

It's a miracle that new fathers readily accept congratulations for doing little more than hanging around a delivery room and getting into everyone's way while trying to remember when it is, exactly, they're supposed to yell, "Push!"

As a child is being born, it seems a miracle that you ever thought there was anything more exciting or fulfilling or important or frightening.

It's a miracle that any human being so purple and wrinkly and messy and loud and demanding, and so closely resembling Edward G. Robinson, can seem so beautiful, and can be so instantly loved.

It's a miracle that, ten minutes after you've been introduced to this new person who's invaded your world, you can barely remember what life was like before you met.

When you come home from the hospital, it somehow seems miraculous that, while your entire life has been suddenly and radically and permanently altered, your house is precisely as messy as when you left it.

It's a miracle that someone soooo tiny who eats soooo little can fill soooo many diapers without going into negative body weight right before your eyes.

And it's a miracle that babies are born with a canny sixth sense that tells them to spit up on your shoulder only when you've forgotten to cover it with a "burp rag."

It's a miracle when new parents who once could sleep through a combination earthquake/nuclear attack are awakened by the absolute silence of a baby who hasn't yet learned that breathing is supposed to be rhythmic.

When you take a newborn baby for a walk, it's a miracle that strangers who normally wouldn't make eye contact with you suddenly turn into old, dear friends who want to hear all the details of your latest accomplishment.

And it's a miracle that while everyone compliments you on how sweet and perfect and wonderful your offspring is, nobody—not a soul—offers to raise it for you.

It's a miracle that even the most curmudgeonly grandfather never, ever says, "Here, you take her for a while."

And it is perhaps the biggest miracle of all when a big brother finally accepts the double standard that, while his new sister gets to stay home all day with Mommy, he still has to go to school. (Of course, it helps when Grandma gives him a box of celebratory cupcakes with pink icing to share with his classmates).

Sob Rule

How to Calm a Crying Baby in 36 Easy Steps

(From the troubleshooting section of *Dr. Dad's Baby Owner's Manual.* Salami Press; $24.95.)

1. Pick up the baby. Maybe he/she wants to be held.
2. Put down the baby. Maybe he/she wants to sleep.
3. Okay. Never mind. Pick up the baby.
4. Rock the baby.
5. Burp the baby.
6. Change the baby.
7. Feed the baby.
8. Feed the baby something no kid can resist, like potato chips, a Three Musketeers bar, or a tall, frosty root beer float.
9. Sing "Rockabye Baby."
10. Sing "I Will Survive."
11. Sing "They're Coming to Take Me Away, Ha Ha."
12. Take baby for a stroller ride around the block.
13. Take baby for a drive around town.
14. Take baby for a plane trip to Walt Disney World and buy him/her several large, expensive stuffed animals.
15. Play "Peekaboo, I See You."
16. Play "This Little Piggie Went to Market."
17. Play hide-and-seek, and hide in a really good place where you can take a minute to pull yourself together.

18. Prove to your baby that, no matter how loud he/she can scream, you can scream twice as loud.

19. Return to your hiding place. You forgot to pull yourself together.

20. Try reasoning with the infant. Say, "Oh, sweetheart, I have so many things to get done. Won't you *please* be quiet and go to sleep?"

21. Try freaking out: "I SWEAR, IF YOU DON'T STOP THIS CATERWAULING RIGHT NOW, YOU CAN JUST PLAN ON MAKING YOUR OWN *&%$# HALLOWEEN COSTUMES!"

22. Return to your hiding place and pull yourself together.

23. Offer baby a cash bribe. Five bucks if he/she stops screaming within the week, ten bucks if he/she stops *today*.

24. Call your baby's doctor. When he says there's nothing to worry about, convince yourself the kid has contracted some horrible, unknown disease, work yourself into a hysterical panic and run into the nearest emergency ward screaming, "Save my child! Save my child!"

25. Return home when it is the majority opinion of 6 doctors, 14 nurses and 32 candy stripers that your baby's only real problem is YOU.

26. Ask your neighbors if they'll watch the baby until he/she falls asleep.

27. Suddenly "remember" that your spouse was just killed in a hunting accident, then ask your neighbors if they could please watch the baby while you're in Montana identifying the body.

28. Tell your neighbors it'll be a cold day in hell before you'll ever do a favor for THEM.

29. Perhaps the baby doesn't like your cologne, deodorant, or personality. So shower, change, and enroll in charm school. Upon graduation, return home and see if the problem persists.

30. Oh, well. Maybe the little darling is ready to sleep.

31. Then again, maybe not.

32. Call Grandma. Remind her how long it's been since she spent any quality time with her new grandchild, and tell her that you're gonna drop the kid off for a nice, leisurely, three-day visit.

33.   Tell Grandma it'll be a cold day in hell before you do any favors for HER.

34.   It's desperation time. You have no choice. Show your baby a picture of Joan Crawford holding a wire hanger.

35.   You animal! Return to your hiding place and pull yourself together.

36.   Hire a live-in nanny and take a two-week vacation in Tahiti. If you return home to find the situation unchanged, build a separate house addition large enough for the nanny and your baby, visit them on weekends, and try to maintain your tan.

Girls! Girls! Girls!

Being a total sports dolt, there was a time when I would have been perfectly happy to sire nothing but girls. Seemed like the perfect sex to me. With luck, I'd never have to show them how to throw a football, explain the rules of ice hockey, or fake my way through a discussion of Wilt Chamberlain's scoring record. On or off the court.

But now that I have a daughter, I occasionally wonder if mandatory sex-change operations for toddlers is such a bad idea. By sheer coincidence, I am sure, this thought springs to mind whenever I'm in the company of my fifteen-year-old niece.

Don't get me wrong. My niece is a great kid, more often than not. And at her absolute worst, she's no more difficult to deal with than the average messy, pouty, lazy, self-possessed, boy-addicted, know-it-all teen princess.

It's that average level of difficulty that frightens me.

(I feel safe in writing frankly about her because she doesn't read anything that isn't about teen rock stars, teen movie stars, teen TV stars, or teen hairdos. If my dust-jacket photo were replaced with a picture of, oh, the cast of "Beverly Hills 90210" or Junior Miss Revlon, I'd be in big trouble.)

Yeah, I'm sure that when my son is fifteen, I'm going to wonder why I wanted to raise anything but a lobotomized eunuch. But as a former adolescent boy myself, I'm at least familiar with the territory. Females are as mysterious to me today as they were in the third grade, when Marla Brickman sent me a mash note during morning recess. By lunchtime she was going steady with Brant Parker and naming the seven children they were going to have together.

Anyway, not long ago, my niece could converse with any adult on any number of topics. Today, however, her vocabulary is exclusively comprised of five words:

1. "Boy(s)"
2. "Buff" (used to describe exceptionally good-looking boys)
3. "Geeky" (unbuff boys)
4. "Guh-rosssssss!" (unbuff boys of exceptional geekiness)
5. Jason (which is, apparently, the name of every boy she knows).

No matter the subject you try to discuss with my niece, all or most of those words will somehow find their way into the conversation. Bring up the signing of the Declaration of Independence, for example, and she will opine that while Benjamin Franklin was geeky, Thomas Jefferson was buff, but even he was guh-rosssss compared to Jason.

There was no escaping this cruel variation of Chinese Water Torture until recently, when the girl's parents had the brilliant idea of installing a private telephone line in her bedroom. Since then, she has emerged only for hair spray, loans, and five-pound bags of double chocolate-chocolate-chip Fudge-a-Rama cookies (the modern teen's primary source of sustenance).

The rest of her waking hours are spent locked in her room, ear to horn, comparing the buffness/geekiness/grossness ratios of her Jason du jour with the Jasons du jour of her girlfriends (all of whom are named Stephanie).

This is a true story. My niece once saw a TV promo for the old late-night movie staple, *The Story of Alexander Graham Bell,* and promptly entered the time and date in her appointment calendar. The inventor of the telephone, she figured, *must* have been buff. Even if he wasn't named Jason.

I don't know if she actually saw the movie, though. She was probably too busy laminating her bangs into what looks to me like a very reasonable facsimile of Grant's Tomb. This is a popular hair style among today's hip and with-it adolescent girls. I like to think it springs from a sense of youthful patriotism, but it's more likely a symptom of an undeveloped mind shellacked in Aqua Net.

For Christmas, my niece's most desired gift was a year's supply of hair spray—and boy, was she thrilled when Santa came through with a full crate of the stuff. She remained thrilled, too, until mid-January, when the supply was exhausted.

God knows what she's using now, but it works. She still looks like she's got a national monument growing out of her skull. I keep waiting for the day she trips and impales somebody with it. Or snags a passing jetliner. I'm telling you, this kid's upper forehead is a disaster waiting to happen.

Oddly enough, my niece's taste in hair styles does not seem driven by peer pressure alone. If she believes in anything, it is in the unparalleled loveliness of her hair. No matter where she is or what she's doing, she will always manage to find *some* reflective surface in which to admire it: a window, a spoon, a plate, a freshly Lemon-Pledged coffee table.

The last time she looked me in the eye during a conversation, I thought, Hey! We're communicating! But no, my mistake. She was just using the reflection in my baby greens to check the altitude and position of her Dippity-Do.

Soon she was back on the phone, gabbing about her latest Jason. And I was at Sports World U.S.A., buying my daughter a football.

The Morning After

'Twas Christmas morning
And all through the house,
There was no room for nuttin',
Not a mouse, not a louse.

My son had been nestled
So snug in his bed
While visions of merchandise
Danced in his head.

Now he'd discover
That dreams *can* come true;
That's the magic of Christmas.
And MasterCard, too.

The boy sprung from his bed
To see what he'd gotten;
If crime doesn't pay,
What about being rotten?

But he saw right away
That St. Nick had come through;
His take stretched from here
To Southeast Timbuktu!

MICHAEL BURKETT

The stocking he'd hung
By the TV with care
Was soon emptied; its contents
Strewn here, there, and there.

Then away to the tree
He flew like a flash,
Tearing into the gift wrap,
Ignoring the sash.

More rapid than lasers
His treasures they came.
He whistled and shouted
And called them by name:

"Here's G.I. Joe trucks!
A Nintendo set! Swell!
And remote-controlled cars
From the folks at Mattel!

"And a gas-powered speedboat
That runs in the tub!"
(Well, it *did*. Till it broke.
Right now it's a sub.)

There were plastic toy figures
So small and petite
That they couldn't be seen
Till they punctured your feet.

And there was a robot;
Wind it up, it'll catch you.

(Well, it *did*. Till it broke.
Right now it's a statue.)

He got musical books
That are battery-run.
They play "It's a Small World"
Till your brain has gone numb.

There was a drum, too,
For the tyke from ol' Santer.
(It was loud. Till I broke it.
Right now it's a planter.)

My son's eyes, how they twinkled!
His dimples, how merry!
Why, this was more stuff
Than Sears, Roebuck could carry!

He was cheering and whooping,
A right jolly young elf,
And I laughed as I watched him
In spite of myself.

He spoke not a word
And kept straight at his duty;
Unwrapping and sorting
And counting his booty.

"And now for the *big* stuff!"
He screamed with delight;
The lad opened his gifties
Well into the night.

MICHAEL BURKETT

By then we were neck-deep
In mountains of boxes,
And undisturbed gift-packs
Of little-kid soxes . . .

And paper and tissue
And ribbons and bows,
And undisturbed gift-packs
Of little-kid clothes.

I turned to his mother,
But I couldn't find her!
Was I to her front,
To her side, or behind her?

We were buried in goods
That were all for our boy;
Every game, every puzzle,
Every book, every toy.

But a squint of his eye
And a jerk of his head
Soon gave us to know
We had something to dread.

The words that he whined
I shall never forget:
"DAAAaaaaaAAAAD!
I didn't get a 'Mad Scientist' set!"

Life Without Father

Blame it on the holidays, the leftover eggnog, or those sappy long-distance telephone commercials on TV, but I've been thinking of calling my father.

It's not like we chat at the beginning of every new year. Or at the beginning of every new decade.

I haven't seen or spoken to the fellow since 1962, when I was thirteen. On that occasion my parents had been divorced six years, and my father made his semiannual appearance at our house to take my sister, my brother, and me out to lunch. I was coming down with the flu, and as soon as our meals were served, I threw up all over the table. And all over the restaurant. And all the way out to his car.

I don't recall actually throwing up *in* his car, too, but maybe I did. That could explain why I never saw him again, even though he lived only fifty miles away.

I did hear from him once more, indirectly, about ten years later. A play I'd written had been produced by a local theater company. My mother sent him copies of the reviews, and he responded by asking for free passes. Maybe it was his idea of a compliment.

I was seven when my mother packed us kids into the family station wagon and dropped my father off—permanently—at his girlfriend's house. All I can remember about him prior to that event is that he called my mother "Toots," he spent most of his free time in our garage, and he once read me a Woody Woodpecker book at bedtime.

I have no recollection of ever calling my father anything but "Buck," which is what everyone else called him. (My mother's name is "Mickey." Growing up, I felt like the child of cartoon characters.) Buck didn't seem to mind this. Heck, it probably made his departure less difficult. I'm sure it's easier to disappear on kids who call you "Buck" rather than "Daddy."

It's surely less rough on the kids, too. I can't imagine myself saying, "Buck! Come home!" without giggling. It sounds like a line from *The Yearling.*

The strangest thing about this threadbare father-son relationship, perhaps, is that I never really minded it. The few times I've thought about Buck, I've thought how weird it was that I didn't think about him more often—or fly into a rage when I did. And unlike my sister and brother, I've never had the impulse to track him down, knock on his door, give him a big bear hug, and start anew wherever it was we left off.

Maybe I've passed on that opportunity because I've always felt it was Buck's responsibility to show up on *my* doorstep. What's more likely, though, is that in some subliminal corner of my brain, I've long imagined any reunion would only confirm my suspicion that, as a father, Buck is no great prize.

No, I'm not dredging this up to treat myself to a warm, nostalgic, postholiday glow. My brother called last night to tell me he'd finally traced Buck's whereabouts and had actually spoken with him on the telephone. Their conversation was pleasant, my brother reported with some surprise, and it ended with Buck requesting that my sister and I give him a call sometime, too.

Well, I thought. The *nerve.* Call *him?* Fat chance. What's the matter? He still hasn't mastered the art of long-distance dialing?

My brother said he'd told Buck what I was doing, that I was married, had two kids, wrote a newspaper column . . . and I could feel my sudden surge of anger give way to primal emotion: Hey! My father's alive! He knows I exist! He knows I have a family! He knows he has grandchildren!

At that moment, for whatever reason, my father seemed important to me. Even though I could barely remember him. Even though I continued to suspect he's a jerk. Hell, I reasoned, he's my *dad*. Lots of dads are jerks.

But after my brother hung up, I reasoned some more. I remembered something I heard Jesse Jackson say on TV years ago: "Any man can be a father, but only a special kind of man can be a dad."

Buck is my father, yes. But is he my dad? No. That title belongs to my mother, my grandmother, and my stepfather—three special people who never disappeared after I threw up, who bought tickets to all my plays (not always a painless task), and who never waited three decades for me to call them.

If I were a member of the Corleone Clan or the Royal Family, I might feel differently. But in my world, it's love, not blood, that's thicker than water.

Bragging Rites

As any parent will tell you, time flies when you're having babies. And it positively zooms when you choose to raise them yourself, as opposed to giving them to friends as a highly personalized, one-of-a-kind gift—an idea that might have worked if I hung out with a slightly dimmer crowd.

It's hard to believe that my daughter is already six months old, and doing something new every time we turn around. This week she's "starting to crawl." This is the tongue-in-cheek term we use to describe her ability to get up on all fours, rock forward and backward, and perform a daring 90-mph face-dive into the floor.

If this kid ever runs away to join the circus, we can at least take comfort in knowing she has an act.

What we're really excited about, though, is that she has already spoken her first words. So far, she's said "vizsla" (which is, according to our Scrabble dictionary, a Hungarian breed of dog), "fraenum" (a connecting form of membrane), and "zeugma" (the use of a word to modify or govern two or more words, while applying to each in a different sense.)

Not only that, she's also started to assemble complete sentences. Just this morning she said, "Iwis cacucha aalii izar phyle." For those without a Scrabble dictionary, this roughly translates into layman's English as, "I would certainly like to perform a Spanish dance under a tropical tree in the fog while dressed in an outer garment worn by Moslem women near a political subdivision in ancient Greece."

We're very, very proud.

She has also reached the stage where any common, nondescript floor covering is viewed as an exotic, all-you-can-eat smorgasbord. This is both a curse and a blessing. Some of the stuff she tries to ingest would gag a seasoned health inspector ... but we haven't had to vacuum for months. I'm thinking of letting her loose in the front yard once a week so we'd never have to mow the lawn.

One thing I'd forgotten about teething babies is that, of all the stuff which squirts, oozes, dribbles, and explodes from their teensy bodies, the substance they produce in greatest volume is drool. Being safety-minded parents, we've instructed our son never to play with his sister unless he's wearing scuba gear. He resisted the idea until our cat drowned in the living room.

Naturally, the boy was distraught. But he perked up when we stocked his bedroom with trout and renewed his fishing license.

Okay. Maybe I'm exaggerating. But we *have* discovered that nothing cleans and shines linoleum quite like generous, repeated applications of fresh baby slobber. No more waxy yellow buildup in *our* kitchen.

My boy, by the way, is adapting well to his bouncing bundle of competition. Lately, in fact, whenever he accuses us of being the meanest parents in the world and threatens to find a more accommodating set of authority figures to live with, he says he's going to take his little sister with him.

I have captured this promise on videotape to freshen his memory when I'm in my fifties and have two teenagers in the house. Until then, I can only pray that I am raising a boy of his word.

Mickey Business

Thousands of years from now, when archaeologists unearth the ruins of my home, they will no doubt assume they've stumbled upon a holy shrine constructed by a small but fanatical sect of cartoon-animal worshipers.

And they won't be far wrong.

I am married to a woman with an insatiable Disneylust—which is much like heroin or cocaine addiction, only a lot more expensive to support. If there are five square inches in our home unoccupied by statues, figurines, music boxes, clothing, or other merchandise stamped with Unca Walt's famous signature-logo, they're hidden by the Disney posters, Disney artwork, and Disney wallpaper.

On the bright side, this woman actually thinks a Donald Duck–emblazoned bottle opener makes for an exciting and thoughtful birthday gift. On the bleak side, it is my suspicion that the main reason she wanted children was so we'd have a good excuse to spend all our vacations at Disneyland.

Pardon me. To the missus, a trip to Disneyland is not a vacation. It is a religious journey. Some families visit the Wailing Wall or the Vatican to celebrate their faith. We go to Pirates of the Caribbean. No matter our actual destination.

A few weeks ago, I mentioned how nice it would be to visit my mother in northern California. My wife's natural response was, "California?! Hey! Disneyland is in California!" Of course, it's also about five hundred miles due south of my mother. But minuscule details like that mean nothing to a Mouseketeer-for-life.

Although I am cynical by nature, I will admit the Disney theme parks offer a one-of-a-kind family adventure. Nowhere else can you plunk down hundreds of dollars for the privilege of being jostled by mobs of rude, testy people; spend more on lunch than you did on airfare; stand in line two hours for a twenty-two-second thrill; take turns marveling over how clean everything is; and strive to get through the day without throttling a short, increasingly cranky loved one.

Those are the things I always remember about Disneyland. But there are others which slip my mind until I return.

Never tell your children in advance that you're taking them to Disneyland. Spill the beans early and they will not sleep from that moment until you pull into the Disneyland parking lot, at which point they will fall into a deep, comalike slumber. Let them snooze and they'll never speak to you again. Wake them up, and they'll behave as if you're dragging them into a forty-eight-acre torture chamber over-run by fuzzy, six-foot cartoon mutants rather than "The Happiest Place On Earth."

Taking an infant to Disneyland is like taking a nun to an orgy: If there is a point, no one knows what it is. Babies don't know Disneyland from Dizzy Dean. And if they did, they still wouldn't give a damn. Yet there isn't a procreator alive who doesn't dream of lashing Li'l Baldy to a rented Magic Kingdom stroller for an entire day.

This, of course, guarantees that at no time will Mom and Dad enjoy the privilege of standing in line two hours for a joint thirty-second thrill. At all times, one baby-minding parent will be benched on the sidelines while the other is driven insane by the baby's older offspring, who aren't quite old enough to understand why they can't go on all the rides at once.

Thanks to an early-childhood trauma, this is not a problem with my son. When he was three, his mother talked him into his very first roller-coaster ride. Alas, the attraction was Disneyland's Space Mountain, a warp-speed hair-whitener that dips and darts through total darkness. The poor kid didn't stop screaming for three days. Even now, all it takes to get him started again are the words "roller," "coaster," "space," "mountain," "fast," or "Mommy," uttered separately or in any combination.

But you've got to give him credit for courage. After two years of refusing to line up for anything but the wimpiest Fantasyland rides, the lad finally mustered the moxie to endure Star Tours, a simulated space adventure inspired by the *Star Wars* trilogy (which just so happens to be his second-favorite movie series after the Godzilla saga). Walking in, you'd have thought he was being led to the electric chair. But walking out, it was clear he'd discovered the happiest corner of the Happiest Place On Earth.

Obviously, my wife experienced a similar transformation years ago. It's just my luck that hers took place in a gift shop.

Sleepy with the Enemy

No matter how much you love babies, there are times when the very last thing you desire is to watch them enjoy their health, happiness, and love of life.

Last night, for me, those times were 11:47 P.M., 12:22 A.M., 1:04 A.M., 1:56 A.M., 2:33 A.M., 3:14 A.M., 4:28 A.M., 5:07 A.M. and 5:49 A.M.... which brings us to yet another entry in the ever-growing *Dad Zone Encyclopedia of Amazing Kid Facts:* Between midnight and sunup, screaming, wet, frightened, vomiting babies are much more adorable than cooing, gurgling, playful babies determined to let the good times roll.

A dead-of-night party atmosphere has pervaded my home for several weeks now and, thus far, I have found only one reliable method of dealing with it. When my daughter's built-in sleep-recess siren goes off—which, by an incredible coincidence, *always* occurs at the exact moment I've finally begun to doze off after the previous alert—I pretend not to wake up.

If I pretend long enough, my wife will eventually rise. At that point, I very sincerely mumble something like, "No, no, honey, it's *my* turn," and pretend to fall back to sleep—effectively absolving myself of guilt, shame, and self-hatred for having no real intention of doing anything but rolling over into a more comfortable position.

Meanwhile, my wife will note that fate has dealt her no choice for the moment but to get up and attempt to convince our princess of darkness that, if this pattern continues any longer, there had better be some screaming and vomiting involved.

Because I am married to such a selfless woman ... or maybe because I'm married to a woman whose brain cells have been tragically depleted due to lack of sleep ... or maybe because I'm married to a woman who has given up on her lazy, worthless jerk of a husband (this is where the smart money is) ... I am allowed to get away with this ruse night after night.

At worst, my wife will return to bed muttering that if MY pattern continues, I can rest assured that there will be screaming and perhaps even some vomiting involved.

Thank goodness women rarely make good on threats made at 2:33 A.M. Otherwise, there would be no such thing as first-year wedding anniversaries and babies who live with their natural parents for more than a couple of weeks.

Still, my wife could become less sweet, selfless, or groggy any moment now. And even if she doesn't, I'm in a quandary which needs to be solved, not merely facilitated.

Pretend sleep is not good enough for me. I require the real REM McCoy—a full, uninterrupted eight to ten hours of it—or I am rendered incapable of articulating the simplest verbs, much less acting them out. Heck, even well-rested I bear a strong resemblance to Slime-O the Semihuman Side-Show Slug, so I cannot afford to skimp in this area.

Besides, my livelihood is at stake here. The column you are now reading has *dozens* of faithful readers. Although most of them happen to be members of my immediate family, they expect and demand top-of-the-line quality (especially Mom). I can't slough off fourth-rate work with the excuse, "Well, whaddaya want? I'm sleepy!"

I've spent many bedtimes trying to get my daughter to understand this. But in her world, apparently, verbs, sleep, rejuvenated brain cells, and fine literature are as unimportant as wake-up calls. She just looks at me with her gap-toothed Lauren Hutton grin and psychically communicates the message, "Tough luck, Dad. I'm a party girl. You'll be hearing from me at 1:56 A.M. By the way, tell Mom it's BYOB."

Photo Fetish

In a merciful world, no parent would be forced to view such horror. But in the flaming hellhole of reality, I had no choice. And it was worse than I ever could have imagined.

My little boy's beautiful, angelic face was frozen, forever, into a grotesque death mask. His huge green eyes were now cruel slashes of black. His smile, once so sweet and hopeful, had been replaced by a hideous grimace.

"Oh, the humanity!" I sobbed. "How much did we pay for these school pictures, anyway?"

I'm not kidding. These were *bad* photographs.

My wife was waiting outside our son's kindergarten classroom the day they were handed out. Upon the last bell of the day, the boy ran to his mother in tears, waving the portrait envelope and wailing, "I'm sorry! I'm sorry! I'm sorry!"

Bear in mind this is a youngster who previously had no idea there was any such thing as good pictures and bad pictures. He thought they were all pretty much the same because he had no standard of measurement.

Well, he now has a standard.

So does his teacher. After class, *she* ran to my wife as well, offering profuse apologies and promising that the new photographs she'd already scheduled to be taken the next week would be far superior to the current batch. That wasn't hard to believe, since the current batch could be used as promotional advertising for *The Night of the Zombie Kindergartners.*

This may sound like a case of common, everyday parental overreaction, but there's a lot at stake here. Consider these sobering facts and figures:

We have approximately 9,762 relatives demanding both wallet-size and eight-by-ten copies of our son's latest school portrait.

Roughly 9,749 of those relatives have never met the boy and have no idea that, in actuality, he's almost as drop-dead gorgeous as his father.

Worse, about 9,718 are getting on in years and could easily expire while under the woeful misimpression that they are blood kin to a five-year-old side-show attraction.

Each of our 9,762 relatives owns a refrigerator and, presumably, refrigerator magnets. This means our son's photo is destined for display all over the country. Should our kinfolk also possess average-size American families (2.8 persons), we're talking 27,333.6 relatives and near-relatives who'd gag at the sight of my kid whenever they passed their own icebox.

If each member of this army welcomed only three visitors per year into their homes within the next year, 82,000.8 total strangers would also come in direct visual contact with the offending portrait.

$$27,333.6 + 82,000.8 = 109,224.4$$

With 86,400 seconds in a day, simple mathematics reveals that every .7902 seconds, someone somewhere in America would be staring slack-jawed at my son's school picture and gasping, "Oh, my! What an unfortunate child!"

And it wouldn't end there. One bad school picture can haunt you forever. Believe me. I speak from experience.

I was home feigning illness the day my fourth-grade pictures were taken. So I posed on another day, for another photographer more fond of extreme close-ups than his predecessor. As it turned out, the picture looked fine—until it was pasted into the school yearbook. Next to all the head-and-shoulder portraits of my classmates, my all-cranium shot made me look like something out of Macy's Thanks-

giving Day Parade. For the next two years, I was known as "Balloon-head Burkett."

Wait. There's more. Thirty years later, I ran into an old grade-school chum. After a very pleasant conversation, he said, "Hey . . . didn't you used to have, like, a really big head? It looks fairly normal now. Did you have surgery or something?"

As you can see, parental overreaction in this situation is impossible. In Japan, I've heard, mothers and fathers commonly kill themselves over bad school pictures as a matter of honor. In some Middle Eastern countries, they simply behead, behand, and befoot the photographer, which seems a much more reasonable solution to me.

But I have no intention of going that far. Not until I see the retakes.

Second Thoughts

I was the second child in my family. Had I been aware of the raw deal I was getting, I might have bribed my older brother to run away from home.

New moms and dads are so awed by the miracle of birth that they're determined to follow through by being perfect parents. But the second time around, they're tired, grumpy, shorter on time than ever before, and determined only to catch as many catnaps as the new kid with the blocks will allow.

In short, their standard of perfection takes a mighty plummet. Examples:

When my son would speed-crawl straight into the furniture, we'd call 911 in a panic, certain he'd suffered a brain concussion. When my baby daughter does the same thing, we consider it cheap family entertainment. Sometimes we phone relatives and neighbors, invite them over, and encourage her to do it again.

Our son wasn't allowed to crawl beyond the perimeter of the freshly washed baby blanket we spread out on the floor for him. My daughter isn't allowed to crawl beyond the perimeter of Maricopa County... unless we're too pooped or too busy to chase after her, in which case she is not allowed to crawl into foreign countries.

We have a complete moment-by-moment photographic record of my son's first five years of life, with multiple copies of each print—

even the badly framed, out-of-focus shots which include portions of our thumbs—just in case we lose the original. For my daughter, we grab the Instamatic only when she does something *really* spectacular, like emerge from the birth canal . . . which, so far, she's done only once.

If our boy threw a temper tantrum while we were in line at the supermarket, we'd buy the kid *anything* to quiet him down as soon as possible. Today we appreciate the fact that nothing thins out a long check-out line more quickly than a shrieking child. We've even considered dangling colorful, unpurchased baubles in front of our daughter to get her going.

Before my son was toilet-trained, his diaper would be changed the second we received the proper visual, aural, tactile, or olfactory signal. With Kid No. 2, we ignore the visual, aural, and tactile signals and change her diaper only when the olfactory signal threatens to render visitors unconscious.

My son wasn't permitted to put anything into his mouth that wasn't approved by Dr. Spock, the USDA, and at least three local pediatricians. My little girl isn't permitted to put anything in her mouth that's on the endangered species list or distinctly labeled with a skull and crossbones.

Whenever my son dropped his pacifier on the floor, we'd dip it in alcohol, boil it in purified water, and zap any remaining germs in the microwave. When my daughter drops her pacifier, we wipe the dirt and cat hair off on our pants and hand it back to her.

My son got a bath a day whether he needed it or not. My daughter gets two washcloth wipe-downs and a good garden-hosing every week, whether she needs it or not. Usually.

MICHAEL
BURKETT

Saving the worst for last:

My son was such a sound, peaceful sleeper we'd often race to his crib in the middle of the night, certain he'd gone into pulmonary arrest. My baby girl snoozes just as quietly... but now we figure that if she *has* gone into pulmonary arrest, we'd be better equipped to deal with it after a good night's rest.

The poor kid.

Hell, poor me.

Road Warriors

When planning family vacations, the normal course of action is to sit down months in advance, scan road maps, study travel guides, and wangle tips from anyone who's ever been outside the city limits.

But parents, in their haste to decide *where* they'll have fun, invariably forget to ask the question that determines *whether* they'll have fun: "Hey, is there some kind of law or something that says we have to take the kids?"

The answer, of course, is absolutely not. And if you're looking forward to an enjoyable, relaxing vacation experience, you'd be wise to exercise your legal and God-given right to find a sucker upon whom you can unload your holy terror(s) pronto.

Relatives are out of the question. You don't want to destroy your relationship with anyone who doesn't slam the door in your face when you show up unannounced and desperate for free childcare. So *think*. Do you know anyone who owes you a huge favor? Perhaps someone whose life you saved. Someone for whom you administered CPR or the Heimlich maneuver, or physically shielded from a volley of machine-gun fire during military service.

If no names spring to mind, you aren't thinking hard enough. Are you a recent blood or organ donor? If so, your generous gift may be keeping a borderline goner from expiring. Track down the lucky recipient, ask how he's feeling, and, no matter how he responds, say, "Well, you'd be dead if it weren't for me, wouldn't you? Speaking of that, what have you done for *me* lately?"

If the fellow isn't a thankless swine, you're on the road to vacation bliss. If he *is* a thankless swine, sorry, pal. You're stuck. All you can do is make the best of a ghastly situation.

Your first step in that direction is to select the proper mode of transportation. Let me warn you in advance that none are very attractive.

Travel by bus, train, or air is prohibitively expensive for most families and, worse, often involves long periods of waiting before departure and during layovers. If there is anything young children do more poorly than wait, the experts have yet to make note of it.

Of those three options, airplanes are most desirable because your travel trauma will be comparatively short, However, crowded jetliners don't offer much in the way of running, jumping, and roughhousing room, and the novelty of zooming through the heavens like Duck Dodgers wears off long before the peanuts are served. Boredom sets in quickly, and most children deal with it by looking for *something* to destroy. This is not acceptable behavior when you're cruising at seventy thousand feet and hundreds of lives are at stake.

Automobiles are your most economical travel option, but what is saved in bucks is lost in sanity. If you're traveling from, say, Los Angeles to Orlando, you're guaranteed to be a twitching, bug-eyed, slobbering fruitcake by the time you reach Pasadena.

Then again, virtually *any* travel adventure with your kids will have that effect. So go ahead and load up the family car.

On the road, your most demanding task will be to keep your children amused. Don't rely on the passing scenery to do the job for you —especially when crossing Texas, Nebraska, and Kansas, where there is no scenery. And don't think you can enthrall them by pointing out roadside attractions during those stretches. Your repeated exclamation of "Look! There's another moo-cow!" will soon prove just as irritating to them as "Are we there yet?" is to you.

Simple rhyming or guessing games can help relieve the back-seat fussiness of preschoolers. Older kids, however, require greater challenges.

One game that will consistently provide you with fleeting moments of peace is "Noise or Cash." Play begins when a parent announces, "I'll give five hundred dollars to the first kid who doesn't make a sound for ten minutes." Don't worry about having to shell out; it's physically impossible for any child to be quiet for ten minutes. But they'll try, over and over again, provided you keep reminding them how much candy and cheap plastic crap five hundred smackeroos can buy.

Long journeys are hard on children accustomed to the freedom of movement and screaming, so be realistic in your expectations of their behavior. For example, kids who squabble incessantly at home aren't likely to call a truce just because they know they'll be terrorizing Chip 'n' Dale in a few days.

If the bickering doesn't cease after several requests, stop the car and explain calmly, clearly, and seriously the kind of behavior you expect. If they fail to deliver, stop the car and explain calmly, clearly, and seriously how dangerous it is for small children to hitchhike from Pasadena to Orlando.

If that doesn't do the trick, pull over one last time, save somebody's life, and pray that he or she will be very, very grateful.

Opposites Detract

In the Superman comic books of my youth, the Man of Steel often hung out in the far reaches of the universe on a cube-shaped planet called Bizarro World, where all the rules of nature, logic, and common sense were reversed. Green traffic lights meant stop, red meant go. Dogs meowed, cats barked. Only those with IQs exceeding that of tapioca pudding were allowed to write television sitcoms. You get the picture.

I have reason to believe that this place actually exists. Furthermore, I am almost certain that my son is from Bizarro World.

This is not a new suspicion. After all, the boy has always responded to the command "Clean up your room" by completely emptying his closets, dressers, and toy box in the middle of the floor. "Be quiet" has always been his cue to improvise a Sensurround production of *The War of the Worlds*. And to his alien ears, "Wash up for dinner" has always meant, "Say! Why don't you see just how filthy you can get in a very short period of time?"

Yes, these were excellent tip-offs to my son's true Bizarro World origins. But I didn't have any solid evidence until last night, when we decided to go out for pizza. The boy asked if he could invite his best pal, Brian, to join us, and I said, "No, not tonight."

Confronted with such parental cruelty, most earthling children can be expected to cry or scream or throw things. Some might even say, "Okay, Dad, you're the boss," while planning to take revenge as soon as they're old enough to borrow your car.

My son, however, chose None of the Above. He ran outside, tracked down his best pal, and hollered, "HEY, BRIAN! WANNA COME HAVE PIZZA WITH US?" As soon as the blood returned to my brain, I called him back inside for a little father-son chat.

"Why did you ask Brian to come when I said, 'No, not tonight'?"

"I . . . I . . . I wanted him to have pizza with us."

"Did you hear me say, 'No, not tonight'?"

"Yes."

"Do you know what 'No, not tonight' means?"

"It means . . . um . . . ahh . . . it means . . . no, not tonight?"

Clearly, he wasn't certain of this. Only on the planet Bizarro World could such uncertainty exist.

"Excellent guess," I said. 'In other words, you heard what I said, you had a pretty good idea what it meant, and you chose to ignore it. Right?"

"Ummm . . . right."

"Well, now you have to go back to Brian's house and tell him you made a mistake and that he isn't invited for pizza after all."

"No! Nooooo! Brian won't like me anymore! NOOOOO! WHAAAAAAAA! Can Brian go have pizza with us? PLEASE, DADDY? PLEEEEEEASE?!?!"

"Sorry," I said, nudging him toward the door. "But if you're not going to listen, you've got to pay the price. Now get over there and tell Brian he is not invited for pizza."

The boy returned a few minutes later with Brian in tow. His spirits were high. Obviously he was proud of himself for bravely correcting his "mistake" and not losing his pal because of it. Needless to say, I was proud, too.

"Hey, Dad," he chirped. "Brian's mom and dad said it's okay for him to go have pizza with us!"

"Yeah," Brian confirmed. "My dad was cookin' hamburgers, but I like pizza better. And I'm hungry!"

How it happened, I don't know. But there I was, at one of those nasty forks in the parenting road where you're damned no matter what you do. I could have destroyed my son's very first best-friendship, hurt Brian's feelings, and made his entire family hate us for life ...or I could have taught my own kid that, yes, indeedy, it *does* pay to ignore your father.

The first option seemed smartest. What the heck. I'd have to live with my son all the way into his adulthood, but I'd be living next door to Brian's family only until we sold our house and moved to another state—which all of a sudden seemed like an imminent and very attractive possibility.

I marched both kids back to Brian's house and explained to his mother what had happened. She was very understanding. Or maybe she just *seemed* understanding in comparison to Brian, who understood only that he'd been double-crossed by dirty, rotten, lying pizza hoarders.

Luckily, children have short-term memories and their forgiveness can be bought with a gift-wrapped slice of double-cheese pepperoni.

Later in the evening, I asked my son if he'd learned anything from his mistake. "Yes, Dad," he nodded. "I learned that going for pizza would be a lot more fun if Brian came with us."

Only a Bizarro Worldian could come up with a moral like that. But we're learning how to deal with the little extraterrestrial. If he ever asks for permission to return to his home planet, we know just what to say: "No, not tonight."

Heh, heh, heh.

Feeding Frenzy

How to Get Baby Food Inside a Baby
in 23 Easy Steps

(More indispensable survival tips from *Dr. Dad's Baby Owner's Manual.* Salami Press; $24.95.)

1.   Accept the grim fact that all babies will eat dirt, rug lint, and old bug carcasses and *like it,* yet very often they'll want nothing to do with the nutritious, scientifically formulated baby foods you try to force down their gullets. This conflict will remain essentially unchanged for the first fifteen or thirty years of your child's life.

2.   Before proceeding with the task at hand, ask yourself: Is this *really* necessary? Is there any way I can manipulate someone else into doing it? Is intravenous feeding out of the question? If your answers are "yes," "no," and "yes" respectively, curse the gods and advance to Step Three.

3.   To ensure a tidy mealtime, gently tie a soft cotton bib around Baby's neck. Then haul the kid to a remote, unpopulated area and deck yourself in one of those heavy-duty rain slickers used by grizzled sea captains during hurricane season.

4.   As you uncap the baby food, describe it in mouth-watering terms an infant can appreciate. Example: "Mmmmmmmmmm! This strained asparagus with tapioca looks even yummier than dirt, rug lint, and old bug carcasses!"

5.   If the target orifice opens wide (in your dreams), take a flying leap to Step Fifteen. Otherwise, adopt an idiotic facial expression and say, "Aw, c'mon, Iddy Biddy Sweedy Pumpkins. Time for din-din!"

6.   Drop the baby talk. You're irritating the child.

7.   Try playing "Open the Hangar, Here Comes the Airplane!"

8.   Try playing "Open the Barn, Here Comes the Horse!"

9.   Try playing "Open the Escape Hatch, Here Comes Lothar, the Brat-Snatching Cyclops from Hell!"

10.   Perhaps your beloved thinks you're trying to poison him/her (and no wonder after that last low-life trick). Taste the food yourself and wait seven or eight hours until the kid is convinced you're suffering no major ill effects.

11.   If Baby remains uncooperative, astound him/her with an incredible true-life fact. Example: "Did you know the South American newt consumes six times its weight in strained asparagus with tapioca EVERY DAY?" When Baby's jaw drops in astonishment, insert loaded spoon. Quickly.

12.   Okay, okay. Some kids are hard to impress. Let's employ the old, reliable "bait-and-switch" sales tactic by waving dirt, rug lint, and old bug carcasses under Baby's nose. Once he/she enters fully gaped crud-intake mode, you're home free.

13.   Apologize to the gods for your rude outburst back in Step Two.

14.   You now have no choice but to exploit the worst and most primal fear of all young children. Dress up like a circus clown, honk a bicycle horn, fall down, hit yourself with a shaving-cream pie, and scream "HI! MY NAME IS GABBO!" The ensuing yowls should give you a clear, unobstructed shot at success.

15.   Are you *sure* intravenous feeding is out of the question?

16.   Hey! the kid is yawning! Quick! Start shoveling!

17.   Phew. You just made it. Now remove the spoon from Baby's mouth with a gentle upward sweep, and DUCK!

18.   Oops. Too late. Hose yourself off and explain to Baby that it's not polite to spit food.

19. Explain the difference between food and finger paints.
20. Explain the difference between food and hair conditioner.
21. Explain the difference between food and full-body mud packs.
22. Mix baby food with dirt, rug lint, and old bug carcasses, dump the whole mess on your living room floor, and let the monster loose. Then wish Baby "bon appetit" as you leave to celebrate the completion of a job well done.
23. Repeat Steps 1 to 22 at next scheduled feeding, which is right about now.

Boy Wonder

The next time you catch yourself griping about some dumb, unimportant thing like the weather or misplaced car keys or a surprise tax audit, think of my brother's twelve-year-old adopted son, Jeremy—the perfect child.

This red-haired, gap-toothed kid operates almost exclusively in three modes: Laughing, Thrilled to Be Alive, and Asleep. Nearly everyone in his small town adores Jeremy. Take the lad for a stroll and total strangers will cross the street to chat with him. Neighbors will run out to the sidewalk with a plate of homemade cookies or, at the very least, greetings so warm and sincere you'd swear they've mistaken Jeremy for their own long-lost son.

The boy is magic.

He is also a victim of cerebral palsy. No, "victim" isn't the right word. Victims hurt. Jeremy laughs. At everything. Make a face or tickle his chin or say grass is purple, and he may become so overcome with joy that he'll wet his pants.

A stroke at birth left Jeremy severely brain-damaged and without the use of his legs, his right hand, and his speech. The doctors said he'd never walk or talk. Jeremy's blood mother apparently believed them.

Today, however, he yaks like one of the Gabor sisters. His "dead" arm is working better than anyone thought it would. Yes, he continues to rely on an electric wheelchair and his adoptive parents' back muscles to get around. But miracles have happened in Jeremy's house before. There could be another.

Okay. Maybe Jeremy isn't really perfect. He requires constant attention. He has a bit of a lazy streak and doesn't always talk as well as he could. Sometimes it's hard to get him to stop laughing long enough to eat his dinner. And, of course, there's those wet pants.

One more thing. While Jeremy is pure joy to be around, he makes me realize how selfish I am. Could I ever take on the 24-hour-a-day responsibility of raising someone else's disabled child? Even THIS child? I don't think so. I seem to have reserved my life's agenda for more important things—though I've yet to determine what those things could possibly be.

Fortunately, selfishness doesn't run in my family.

When my brother, David, married his wife, Norma, in 1981, she was already the mother of two boys and an adopted girl. Still, they decided there was room for one more. David had worked professionally with the disabled for fifteen years and had long wanted to adopt a handicapped child. Norma's interest began with her first boyfriend. "He didn't have any arms. I was fascinated by him. Not by what he couldn't do, but what he *could* do."

Their first move toward adoption, Norma recalls, was to visit a home for disabled children "to see how they'd react." When Jeremy (then two) was brought out, they all dropped to their knees and started playing with him. The attendant said, "This one's gonna be yours."

But David and Norma already knew.

"People always ask, 'Why did you adopt a handicapped child?'" Norma tells me. "Well, in many ways, Jeremy has been easier to raise than my other children. He's very independent now, but at one time you could put him somewhere and you'd know he'd stay put. When you've chased after three normal kids for eighteen years, you can't help but think, 'Hey! This ain't bad!'

"And when you have a normal child, you miss so much because you take every progression for granted. With Jeremy, each new step is so significant and thrilling—an incredible little victory."

I hate to ask, but... what if Jeremy stops progressing?

"I don't know," my brother concedes. "Sometimes when I pick him up, I think, 'My God! He's a hundred pounds and I'm forty-four years old! When he's another hundred pounds and I'm sixty-four, what am I going to do?' But there's only one thing I *can* do," he laughs. "Gotta keep myself in shape."

"There's no limit to the things any parent can worry about," Norma says. "But it always boils down to this: Give 'em your best and hope for the rest."

I may never find my name on anyone's list of the world's greatest parents. But it's great to know I'm related to two very qualified candidates. And Jeremy, the near-perfect child.

Look Who's Thinking

What do babies think? Due to an incredible scientific breakthrough accomplished with the newest and most sophisticated brain-wave analysis devices, it is now possible to literally read the minds of infants.

Despite the potential "brain drain" risks reported in a recent *Newsweek* cover story (one test child was rendered so mindless he is now mistaken almost daily for Maury Povich), I allowed my seven-month-old daughter to undergo a "head read," conducted in her natural environment. Here are the results.

Oooh! Look at that! I don't know what it is, but I'm gonna try to eat it . . .

Hey! What was I doing? I forget. I hate it when that happens. Oooh! Look at that! I don't know what it is, but I'm gonna try to eat it . . .

Where was I? Oh, yeah. I was gonna scale our home entertainment center. Now if I can just hoist myself up on this wire . . . Nope. No good. Maybe if I wrap it around my neck thusly . . .

Whoooops! Hey! I'm flying! Just like Superbaby! Flying through the skies to save the world from total destruction! I'm flying into . . . Oh, no! My playpen?! WAAAAAAAAAAAAAAH! Help! Save me! WAAAAAAAH! NOT THE PLAYPEN! NOT THE . . .

Oooh! Look at that! I don't know what it is, but I'm gonna try and eat it . . .

Uh-oh. There's that rumbling noise. Maybe it's a false alarm . . . Nope! It's a mud slide! Run for your lives! WAAAAAAAH!

Phew. Mom showed up just in time. I was almost buried alive... EEEYOW! Where you been keepin' those baby wipes? In the deep-freeze? Next time, how about chippin' the ice off 'em first?

Hey! I'm flyin' again! Wheeeee! Superbaby! Flying into...my crib? No! No! I'm not sleepy! Really! Heck, if I was sleepy, I wouldn't have the energy to do this: WAAAAaaaaHHHHHHhhhhHHHH! Or, for that matter, this: WAAAAAAAaaaaaHHHHHHHaaaaaHHHHHHHHaaahhh HHH! Now lemme outta here! Mom? Mom? Zzzzzzzzzz...

Huh? Where am I? Hmmm. Still in bed. Mom must have knocked me unconscious and left me here, trapped like a rat. Maybe I can climb out. Ooooh, look at that! I don't know what it is, but I'm gonna try to eat it...

Hey! There's Dad? He'll bust me outta this joint!...Hey, Dad, where ya going? You forgot to pick me up! WAAAAAHHHHHHHHHHHH! Ha. It worked. What a sucker.

Hiya, Dad. You know, you'd be a pretty good-lookin' guy if you didn't have all that hair on your face. Here, lemme rip it off for you with my world-famous vise grip...Oh, calm down. Lemme try again, using both hands...Okay! Okay! I'll just yank out one hair at a time... Sheesh. What a wimp. How about I just sink my dainty little razor-sharp fingernails into your face?...

WHOOOOPS! I'm flyin' again! No! NOOOOO! Not back to the play-pen! WAAAAAHHHHHHHHHHHH! Oooh, look at that! I don't know what it is, but I'm gonna try to eat it...

Hmmm. I'm famished, and this mystery food ain't helping. Time to ring the dinner bell. WAAAAAAAHHHHHHHHHHHHH!

Joy of joys. Here comes Mom with some eats. What's on the menu tonight, Mom?...Wow! Strained peas! My favorite! Gimme a big ol' honkin' spoonful. Mmm-mmm, good!

Say, Mom, now that my mouth is full of strained peas, wanna see my impression of an outboard motor? Watch this. It's great. PFFFFFFFFFFFFFHHHHHH! Not bad, huh?

Hey! Where'd the peas go? And where did this bottle come from? I don't want no stinkin' bottle. Here, I'll demonstrate by throwing it on the floor. See?

What are you doin'? Don't pick it up and give it back to me! Obviously, you're confused, so let's go over it one more time. When I throw my bottle THUSLY, it means "Ixnay on the ottlebay." Got that? In other words, more strained peas! More strained peas! More strained...

Whoooops! Superbaby is flyin' back to the living room floor! Well, it's about time! Let's see. What was I doing before all those rude interruptions? Oh, yeah. I was scaling the home entertainment center. Now, where's that wire?...

Oooh! Look at that! I don't know what it is, but I'm gonna try to eat it....

Multiplication Lessons

Life is never the same once you start reproducing. Everyone knows that. But most folks base their baby-making decisions on the big changes you can see from a mile off—like increased responsibility, decreased personal freedom, complete financial ruin, and the loss of once-valued friends who start asking if that new cologne you're wearing is called Eau de Diaper Pail.

What future moms and dads fail to consider, due only to lack of experience, are the trillions of tiny, day-to-day life changes which actually define parenthood.

Welcome to the tip of the iceberg.

For the first three or four years of your child's life, simple trips to the grocery store for a single loaf of bread will require roughly as much preplanning, supplies, and physical agility as a six-month mountain-climbing expedition to Nepal.

For the first eighteen years of your child's life, you will never, ever, ever, ever, ever, ever, ever oversleep. Ever.

The nicest compliment you will receive concerning your personal appearance is, "My! You don't look nearly as exhausted today as you did yesterday!" And you'll be thrilled to hear it.

You will be consistently astounded by your own sincerity as you look at a formless mass of crayon scribbles and exclaim, "Oh, how pretty! You're really turning into quite the little artist!"

You will forget what silence sounds like. And if for one brief, unlikely moment you are ever reminded, you will automatically fly into a panic and assume your children have been kidnapped.

Your appreciation of naps will increase in direct proportion to your child's inability to understand why he shouldn't wake you up to help him find his water pistol.

While reading the morning paper, some primal self-defense mechanism in your brain will beg you to skip over any news story involving children. If you ignore this warning, you will be sorry.

You will not remember the lyrics to any songs except "It's a Small World," the "Sesame Street" theme, and "Under the Sea." In fact, you will not remember that any other songs exist.

At video stores, you will rent six tapes for your children and one for yourself, hoping you won't be too tired to watch it once the kids are in bed, which never happens.

You will forget that the major Hollywood motion picture studios continue to produce movies about living, breathing human beings *in addition to* movies about cute, anthropomorphized cartoon animals.

On good days, you won't be able to look at someone else's children without smugly comparing them to your own kids, who are much cuter and smarter.

On bad days, you won't be able to look at someone else's children without wondering if you were the victim of a hospital baby-switch.

While driving, you will constantly adopt a silly, high-pitched voice to say things like "Look! A great big horsie-worsie!" before remembering the kids aren't in the car.

When you want to see the latest touring production of the Broadway musical Cats, you will instead see the latest grade-school production of the original musical *Sing! Sing! Sing About Spring!* And afterward, you will very seriously wonder why they don't hand out Tony Awards for Best Cameo Performance by a Bumble-Bee.

Whenever you enter a sit-down restaurant with the kids in tow, the waitress will demand her tip in advance and *still* treat your family like plague-bearing weasels. When you tire of this, you will restrict your patronage to dining establishments where all meals include a toy.

Your first child will be allowed to officially name every living creature in your home, until he suggests that his new baby sibling be dubbed "Bigfoot."

You will realize that the most beautiful words in the English language are "I love you, Mommy and Daddy" . . . and that the second most beautiful words in the English language are "Congratulations! Your child is eligible to attend summer camp!"

Home on Derange

A recent government study concluded, after years of exhaustive research, that husbands cook fewer family meals than their wives. Obviously, this project was funded by the kind of freeloading, Fed-funded Einsteins who would surmise, after years of exhaustive research, that men are more likely than women to suffer from jock itch.

Rare are the husbands who know Spic 'n' Span from Frick 'n' Frack. And those who do are almost always useless when it comes to performing traditional American-guy tasks—like spending three days crawling around under a dead car before hauling it off to someone who might actually know how to fix it.

Being a traditional American guy, I consider slobbiness a part of my personal style. My wife learned this about me on our third date, when I had finally succeeded in luring her to my bachelor pad. Her first comment upon entering was that I should put a welcome mat *inside* the door so I wouldn't track filth into the street.

Back then, she must have assumed my swingin'-single lifestyle was so exciting and action-packed that I didn't have time for menial chores like dusting, waxing, and harvesting the mushroom patch in the back of my refrigerator. But now that we're married and have thrown two kids into the picture—which somehow octuples the average household mess—she is not so much charmed as perpetually irritated.

Clearly, we have a problem here, and it's up to me to take care of it. Yes, it's high time I bit the bullet, put my nose to the grindstone, sat my wife down, and got her to accept certain ugly, inescapable truths about us traditional American guys.

It's going to be a challenge. First off, this is a female who refuses to believe that it's physically impossible for a man to walk through a bathroom without leaving a thin layer of tiny little hairs all over the sink—a natural phenomenon beyond our control, as any trustworthy member of my sex will tell you.

My wife also seems to think that by simply asking me to put my dirty dishes in the dishwasher instead of the sink—or in the sink rather than on top of the TV—she's going to miraculously overrule the millions of years of male genetic memory that subliminally command me to put them in the first empty space I find.

I don't mean to imply that all male behavioral patterns in this area are inbred. Some are simply the product of our foolproof logic and scientific acumen.

Men know, for example, that bacteria breed much like all other life forms, and that there's no better way to reduce their population than by keeping the little suckers apart. This explains why we spread our dirty clothes all over the house rather than lumping them in the clothes hamper—a veritable Sodom and Gomorrah for horny, microscopic vermin.

Male logic knows no household bounds. The most common complaint by women about their mates, of course, is that whenever a man exits the bathroom, the toilet seat is invariably left in the upright position. To the masculine mind, this is far more thoughtful than at least one alternative, which is to leave the toilet seat down...and damp. Why women don't *thank* us for lifting the damn thing is an unsolved mystery worthy of Robert Stack.

While we're on the subject of the unexplainable, my wife read about that government study I mentioned earlier, and concluded that I should start preparing more of the family meals. Even though she's tasted my cooking. Even though she remembers the night I formulated "Spork 'n' Beaghetti Mexicali," a zestful blend of leftover spaghetti and pork and beans, dumped into one big bowl and served with a bag of Fritos.

Not long ago, after being left to my own devices for the evening, I was subjected to all sorts of grief for giving my son a bowl of raisin bran for dinner. Now, really. What was so bad about that? Raisin bran is fortified with ten essential vitamins. It contains fruit, whole grains, and milk to build strong bones. Plus, it's an effective aid against irregularity. You can't say that about most of the meals my wife prepares.

"Cooking isn't *that* hard," my wife grumbles. "You could use the microwave."

Apparently, she doesn't know that raisin bran is already cooked. Nor will she believe that all I can accomplish with a microwave is to make food inedible in a shorter period of time—a feat that amazes me but does not impress my son. Especially when he's hungry, Mom isn't due home for a few hours, and we're fresh out of raisin bran.

And it's not like I *never* cook. I do. I barbecue. This traditional, American-guy mode of food preparation involves only one, easy-to-remember rule: When it's not too black, it's ready to eat. While that dictum applies very nicely to hamburgers and steaks, however, it does not apply to tuna casserole, frozen pizzas, or TV dinners. Believe me.

Frankly, my wife may not be ready to acknowledge the God-imposed limitations of husbands like myself. But I have a back-up plan. When logic and reason and history fail me, I'll offer to whip up another batch of "Spork 'n' Beaghetti Mexicali."

And if that doesn't work? Maybe I'll try altering the course of American-guy history by putting my dishes in the sink.

Mean Cuisine

I have received so many letters from harried househusbands requesting the complete recipe for "Spork 'n' Beaghetti Mexicali" that I offer it here—along with a few other Dad-tested creations which require little or no time, effort, or culinary talent.

Spork 'n' Beaghetti Mexicali

The perfect meal for those days when your kids just won't stop screaming, "Starch! Starch!" And the beauty part of this recipe is that everyone has the ingredients right in their own kitchens! What you'll need:

    1 can pork and beans
    1 plastic Tupperware bowl of leftover spaghetti
    1 bag Fritos
    1 ice cream scoop.

DIRECTIONS: Dig through the back of your refrigerator for the Tupperware bowl of leftover spaghetti. (Don't give up; it's back there somewhere.) Using the ice cream scoop, remove as much mold as possible. Add pork and beans and Fritos. Salt to taste, or salt to *obliterate* taste. Serves one to as many people who'll touch it.
NOTE: Leftover Spork 'n' Beaghetti Mexicali (pardon the redundancy) makes an excellent Show-and-Tell Project for grade-schoolers.

Raisin Bran Surprise

Ask any parent. There's only one thing children love more than raisin bran... and that's a surprise! They get both with this delicious and versatile conversation-starter—at breakfast, lunch, or dinner! What you'll need:

1 cup Raisin Bran
½ cup milk
½ teaspoon white sugar
1 surprise (a slice of Spam, a plastic tarantula, some leftover Spork 'n' Beaghetti Mexicali, or whatever's handy that no one would expect to find in their raisin bran).

DIRECTIONS: Place "surprise" at bottom of bowl. Add Raisin Bran, milk, and sugar. Serves one until he or she discovers the Lucky Prize.

Hot Raisin Bran Surprise

Microwave above concoction on high for two minutes, stir, and serve. (WARNING: If the "surprise" is explosive, made of metal, or alive, remove prior to cooking.)

Multitemperature Raisin Bran Surprise

Same as above, but don't stir.

Raisin Bran Surprisicles

Stick a spoon into Raisin Bran Surprise, freeze, remove from bowl, and serve.

N'Mores

Are your kids wolfing down too many between-meal snacks? Or are you just too darned tired or busy to keep scouring your pantry for something they'll eat? Either way, you can curb their appetites with this variation on the ever-popular "S'Mores," which I invented during a household marshmallow shortage. What you'll need:

1 package graham crackers
½ pound melted chocolate
1 can oil-packed tuna fish.

DIRECTIONS: You get the picture. I'd rather not think about it any more, thank you very much. Serves none.

156

The Official Toxic Avenger Squeeze-Tube Dessert Stick

Hey, Dad! Don't toss those old, black, shriveled-up bananas just because their innards have turned into a gelatinous brown goo! Turn them into a fun and healthy meal-topper inspired by every young boy's favorite Saturday-morning cartoon show! What you'll need:

1 extremely overripe banana
1 pair scissors.

DIRECTIONS: Take the banana, the scissors, and the kid outside. Cut off one tip of the banana, hand it to Junior, and tell him to *squeeze*. Serves one. All over the neighborhood.

A Pox Upon Me

My son calls it "chicken pops," as if it were a new poultry-flavored brand of breakfast cereal. But the truth is, chicken pox is worse than that. If you can imagine such horror.

The worst part of this highly contagious kiddie disease is not that it makes your children look like the tragic victims of an Oxy-10 shortage, or that they aren't allowed to attend school or play with their pals or venture outside for the short eternity it takes for their bodily complexions to clear up.

No, the main reason to dread chicken pox is that, more often than not, its victims remain healthy enough to whine "I'M BOOOooo-OOORED" every time they exhale. It was this characteristic, I'm sure, that inspired the ancient curse, "a pox upon your family."

It may also explain why Mother Nature—or Uncle Vermin or whoever's responsible for such things—arranged it so children only get this bug once per lifetime. No quarter-sane parent would put up with it *twice*.

Kids get chicken pox the same way they get popular, ghastly new toys you're determined never to allow in your house. First you hear the thing is sweeping the nation. Then a youngster down the street gets it. Then every child on your block follows suit. And before you know it, one of your own little darlings brings it home to share with his siblings.

Given the choice, you're better off with a kid who's feigning illness than one who's poxed—but not for the obvious humanitarian reasons.

You see, the fakers know that if they don't maintain the illusion of being near death, they risk an immediate return to household slavery. But kids with chicken pox *love* to flaunt the fact that thay feel pretty good, they're missing school, they've fouled every square inch of the house, they've reduced you to a slobbering shadow of your former self... and there's nothing you can do about it but cater to their every whine.

Yep. The moment your beloved's first bright red splotch has been lovingly swabbed with calamine lotion, you are no longer a parent. You become the world's lowest-paid, least-appreciated entertainment director. And no matter your level of creativity or enthusiasm, you *will* fail at this job.

You can haul out the crayons and the coloring books and the Play-doh and the construction paper; rent every violent, poorly animated kid video on the market; say "Hey! Wanna play *another* game of 'Uncle Wiggly'?" 'til the cows come home; hire Siegfried and Roy to perform in your living room ... and your child will continue to behave like the victim of gross parental neglect.

According to the experts, chicken pox is a fairly harmless affliction unless your child displays any "abrupt mental changes." So naturally, I panicked when my son was suddenly overcome with the desire to go outside, track down some playmates, and actually participate in his own life.

Leaving the house is usually the last thing he wants to do. Outside there's no TV, no dinosaur fruit snacks, no toys of destruction directly underfoot, no mothers or fathers or sisters to annoy.

Yet there was my polka-dotted prepubescent, acting like a hopeless nature addict in the advanced stages of fresh-air withdrawal. It just goes to show what a raging 98.7-degree fever can do to an undeveloped human brain.

Ah, well. We've had it easier than most of the parents in our heavily blemished neighborhood. Chicken Pox Rule Number One is to prevent your kids from scratching their blisters into gaping wounds, and that's been no problem for us because my son has seen enough violent, poorly animated kid videos to equate even the tiniest amount of blood with instant death.

(This notion takes a lot of the worry out of child-rearing; ours is not a boy who's ever going to come home with a tattoo, a pierced nose, or a body part lopped off during a poorly played round of mumblety-peg.)

Happily, the lad has recovered to the point where he now answers to the nickname "Scabby Hayes." But my daughter is starting to look a little blotchy, and all of a sudden she doesn't want to do anything but go outside and play.

Pardon me while I prop open the front door.

Ice Scream

There is no limit to the sacrifices parents will make for their children. Sometimes they are forced to kill. Sometimes they are forced to die. And sometimes they are forced to attend Walt Disney's World on Ice.

At first, I was excited when my wife told me she'd purchased a family pack of tickets to see "Disney on Ice." I mean, how often do you get the chance to view the cryogenically frozen remains of an honest-to-goodness cultural icon like Walt Disney?

"No, no, no, no," my wife said, her patience dwindling a mere six seconds into the conversation. (The longer you're married, the less time such things take.) "It's an ice show. Like the Ice Capades, only with Disney characters."

If I have ever been more disappointed, the experience was so emotionally scarring I have blocked it from memory.

The first and last time I attended the Ice Capades, I was about seven years old. Even at that tender age it seemed a monumentally silly form of entertainment: people in gowns and tuxedos skating around in circles while the audience members teeter on the edge of their seats, wondering if someone might—gasp!—slip, fall, and get ice chips in his or her perfectly coiffed hair during the course of the performance.

Now, that may qualify as real knuckle-whitening, heart-stopping excitement for some folks, but not me. And I seriously doubted that the suspense would be heightened by a bunch of Winter Olympic washouts dressed up like cartoon mice, ducks, and chipmunks.

But hey. I'm a dad. My son wanted to go, and by God, I wasn't gonna let him down. When you're a dad, you're a dad, and you've got to play the role even when it goes against your moral, ethical, and entertainment values.

A father's first task upon approaching the gates of Walt Disney's World on Ice, I found, is to shell out nine bucks for a battery-powered Mickey Mouse light sword. The outdoor concessionaires announce via bullhorn that it is virtually impossible to enjoy the show without one ... while the indoor concessionaires announce via bullhorn that it is virtually impossible to enjoy the show without *two.*

(As it turns out, there is indeed a limit to the sacrifices a parent will make for his child, and eighteen dollars is it.)

In retrospect, I can see that it is sheer folly to hand a six-year-old boy a battery-powered Mickey Mouse light sword and expect him to keep it sheathed and unlit for two hours. No, he's gonna turn that sucker on, raise it over his head, and inform the world, *"I am the Dragonmaster!"*

He will then commence to scream, *"Aha! You die!"* while swinging his weapon at everyone he sees—which can be a pretty time-consuming activity when you're in a stadium filled with about ten thousand hyperactive children who think *they* are the Dragonmaster.

Eventually, my son settled down, but at no point did he become more fascinated with the show than he was with his brand-new light sword. And frankly, that was not difficult to understand.

The show was simply a rinky-dink re-creation of Disney's *Peter Pan* movie, which my son has seen a few million times on videotape —and which seems an odd choice of material for an ice-skating show, since the characters spend so much of their time flying. I don't care how good a skater you are, there aren't many stunts you can perform while dangling from a wire, thirty feet in the air. Unless flailing your arms and legs qualifies as a stunt. In a world where ice shows qualify as entertainment, anything is possible.

The show didn't improve much when the performers were on the rocks, so to speak, because they rarely stopped singing morbidly cheerful tunes with lyrics like, "Everything free and easy, do as we darn well pleasey." During these musical interludes, it was all I could do to keep from grabbing my son's light sword, storming the rink, and screaming, "Aha! You die!"

But I didn't. For one thing, my son wasn't about to part with his weapon. For another, it is my firm conviction that parents who behead cartoon characters in front of their children are setting a very poor example indeed.

Alas, good examples are wasted on my son. During the climactic finale of Walt Disney's World on Ice, I turned to see if he'd ever gotten caught up in the action. "Dad," whispered the Dragonmaster with a malevolent grin, "I'm gonna cut your arms off."

He didn't make good on the threat, thank heavens. But under the circumstances, the loss of a limb or two would have seemed a minor sacrifice.

162

Mom's the Word

It may be the worst trade-off since Manhattan Island was sold for junk jewelry. Our mothers give us two lifetimes—theirs and ours—and we give them one crummy Sunday a year. Zowie.

The epic scale of this gyp became clear to me a few years ago, when Mom and I were waxing nostalgic about what a delightful child I had been and reeling over how lucky she was to produce *me* in only one out of three tries.

Actually, Mom wasn't waxing and reeling so much as rolling her eyes and making rude gagging noises. But I was definitely in golden-memory mode. And it finally seemed as if sufficient eons had passed to confess the Greatest Triumph of My Youth without getting sent to my room, whacked upside the head, or getting grounded for life.

I was in junior high school at the time, determined to stay home the next day in order to avoid some long-forgotten horror (a test, a schoolyard beating, a zit the size of Herve Villechaize).

My plan seemed foolproof from the start. I got up in the middle of the night, took my bedroom wastebasket into the kitchen, and proceeded to fill it with raw eggs, refried beans, creamed corn, leftover lasagna, vinegar, cottage cheese, a couple of Alka-Seltzer tablets (for that all-important bubble-effect), and anything else I could find to create two gallons of the most realistic fake vomit this side of Repulsive Novelty Items R Us.

The next morning I brilliantly recreated Yul Brynner's death scene from *The King and I* while pointing—ever so weakly—to the artificial upchuck. Lemme tell ya, it was a glorious start to a glorious day of TV game shows, soap operas, Captain Hook's Kartoon Kavalcade and "The Four-Star Afternoon Movie."

So glorious that some thirty years later, when I let Mom in on the ingenious scam, I was sure she'd sprint directly to the phone and call all her friends to brag about the cunning child she'd raised.

"Idiot," she muttered. "I knew you were faking it. I was a *nurse,* for heaven's sake."

Why did she let me stay home?

"Because any kid who'd go *that* far to get out of school for one day must have a good reason."

At that moment, I realized my search for a really cool parental role model was over. I'd had one in my own family for years and never knew it.

Of course, if I were truly cunning, I'd have started appreciating this woman long ago. Like when she'd let me go to the movies on a school night for the premiere of the latest Steve "Hercules" Reeves adventure, because she knew I'd curl up and *die* if I wasn't the first kid on my block to see it.

Or when my high school principal summoned both of us to his office and asked if that was *her* signature on the fifteen or twenty absentee notes spread out before us. It wasn't. But on the way home, Mom didn't rant or rave or threaten to ship me off to a military academy. She didn't have to. (From then on, I forged her signature only when it was absolutely necessary.)

For better or worse, it was Mom who influenced me to become a writer instead of a cartoonist, which was my career goal at the age of ten. Every day I'd show her my latest drawing, and she would always respond with praise and encouragement. So when I took my first stab at prose with the heartwarming tale of a boy and his radioactive, sister-eating warthog, I expected a similar reaction. Instead, Mom politely suggested that I go back to the drawing board. Literally and as soon as possible.

Being a teen-rebel-in-training, I had no choice but to trash my colored pencils and rework the warthog saga into a novel. (Mom doesn't remember this incident, but she continues to ask if I've drawn any cartoons lately.)

Like all kids, I thought my mother possessed a cruel and inhumane sense of justice. Once, as my brother and I were doing the dishes, we got into a sword fight with Mom's brand-new carving knives and nicked the blades so badly they couldn't slice hot Jell-O. Our awful punishment? We were forbidden to watch our favorite TV hero, Zorro, cross blades with his enemies for TWO WHOLE WEEKS!

Mom was so upset it didn't occur to her that the thirty-minute program was broadcast just once a week—adding up to a full hour's discipline for destroying seventy-eight dollars' worth of cutlery. But I don't think I really forgave her until she admitted her role in The Greatest Triumph of My Youth.

No wonder "Mom" spelled upside-down is "wow."

Grody to the Max

There. Now that we've sent the pantywaists packing, let's discuss what the early stages of parenting are really like. The everyday details of child-rearing you never read about in daily newspapers.

To illustrate: I recently went to give my baby daughter a good-night kiss and, just as our lips met, she threw up. I'm not talking about dainty baby-spit. I'm talking about a full-scale recreation of Linda Blair's dampest scenes from *The Exorcist.*

Not long ago, my reaction to such an event would have been to scream in disgust while racing to the shower. But as all parents soon discover, when it's your own poor, sickly flesh and blood doing the projectile spewing, the picture changes entirely.

As I stood there with my daughter's dinner dripping from my beard, my first thought was, "Oh, my own poor, sickly flesh and blood!" My second thought was, "Where's the thermometer?" My third thought was, "I hope we've got clean sheets." That's how my dad brain clicked until she was fast asleep.

Amazing. Prior to fatherhood, if someone had told me, "One day someone will throw up in your face and you won't mind," I wouldn't have believed him. Even if he said the vomiter was a close relative.

Nor could I have been convinced there'd come a day when I'd regularly *volunteer* to hold a Kleenex to somebody else's nose, and that this person would regularly blow, miss the tissue entirely, and give me a handful of semifluid that would make Jean-Claude Van Damme scream in disgust while racing to the shower.

Or that the cry "I'm done!" would compel me to stop whatever I was doing, make a beeline for the commode, and swab up after somebody else's personal business.

Not only do moms and dads think nothing of dealing with their child's southernmost eliminations on an hourly basis, they become, early on, positively obsessed with them. Every diaper load is regarded as an up-to-the-minute health report.

Here's how bad it can get. In homes without babies, the average husband-wife conversation goes something like this:

"Honey, I'm home!"

"Hello, dear. How was your day at the office?"

"Awful. Boy, am I glad to be home. Where's the *TV Guide*, blah blah blah..."

Throw an infant into that scenario and it unfolds thusly:

"Honey! How's his poop?"

"I'm worried. It's a little dark."

"How dark? Burnt-almond dark or café-au-lait dark?"

"I think it was more of a Sicilian umber."

"Geez. I hope it's milk-chocolate by tomorrow."

"Let's wake him up. Maybe if we bounce him around for a while he'll poop again."

Such dialogues are not limited to the privacy of home and hearth. They take place everywhere fledgling moms and dads go. Their babies have become their world, and poop-monitoring has become their reason to live. They no longer have hobbies or outside interests or friends. Until the successful completion of toilet training, NOTHING ELSE MATTERS.

This may explain why new parents are rarely invited anywhere. Who wants to host a party where half the guests are comparing their childrens' gastrointestinal output as the other half screams in disgust while racing to the shower?

It's a lonely business, parenting.

Tick ... Tick ... Tick ...

One minute is such a relative length of time.

For example:

Stick a frozen turkey in the microwave, hit the high button, and sixty seconds later you'll still have a frozen turkey. Do the same thing to, oh, a live frog, and you'll alter its molecular structure. All over your kitchen.

Major life changes can be made in one minute. You can decide to quit your job, chuck everything, change your identity, and move to another country. But in the next minute, you may not be able to decide if you're in the mood for Chinese food or Italian.

In one minute you can drive a mile—unless you're commuting on the Los Angeles freeway system between the hours of 4 A.M. and 11 P.M., in which case you can drive nowhere at all.

Get trapped in an elevator with George Burns, Audrey Hepburn, Gregory Peck, Katherine Hepburn, Jimmy Stewart, Sharon Stone, Nolan Ryan, Paul Newman, Robin Williams, or Cindy Crawford for a single minute, and you'll wish time would stop.

Get stuck in the same elevator with Howard Stern, Geraldo Rivera, Shelley Winters, Bobcat Goldthwaite, Chuck Woolery, Tom and Roseanne Arnold, or David Duke, and you'll soon be convinced, beyond any doubt, that time *has* come to a screeching halt.

While visiting old friends, minutes shrink to milliseconds. But when you're at a party where you don't know a soul and everyone would like to keep it that way, each minute ticks off like a long, hot summer.

Roger Bannister could run a quarter mile in one minute. Certain others—whimsically referred to as "fast-food employees"—can't carry a quarter-pounder a quarter-inch in a quarter-hour.

For one minute, imagine yourself changing a flat tire in Death Valley at high noon, downtown Detroit at midnight, or Fresno, California, at any time of day. And then for the next minute, picture yourself anywhere else, doing anything else.

Quite a relief, eh?

Great and complex scientific conclusions have been formulated in one minute. Yet within the same time frame, some folks can't figure out how to operate a corkscrew or get through a revolving door.

A minute feels like forever when you're being held down and tickled. But if you're being held down and kissed, it hardly exists. Unless you're being kissed by someone you don't like. Then it feels like forever again.

There is, too, the minute we read about every morning, every summer, in almost every newspaper in the country. You know the one. The "I-only-turned-my-back-for-a-minute" minute.

It is during this tiny chunk of eternity that parents are distracted by one insignificant thing or another as their child wanders into the back yard, falls into the swimming pool they'd always meant to kid-proof, and drowns or is permanently brain-damaged.

That is the fastest minute there is. But it lasts a lifetime. A lifetime of horror, loss, heartbreak, guilt, regret, and pain that never lets up.

Not for a minute.

Not for any minute.

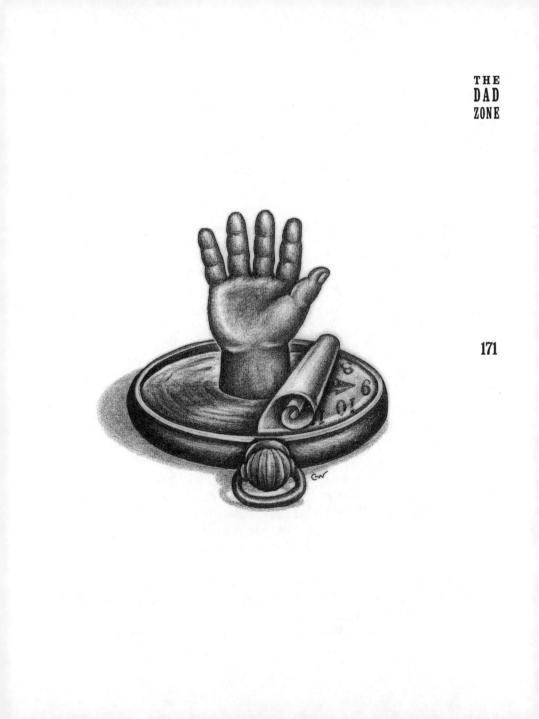

Killer Kisses

Every night, without fail, my son stalks me down for a good-night kiss. What's nice about this ritual, other than the smooch itself, is that it's something he's *wanted* to do ever since he could muster a pucker.

At bedtime, we have to fire up the cattle prod to get the boy to pick up his toys or brush his teeth or make one last trip to the bathroom, which he fights even when his bladder is threatening to explode like the *Hindenburg*. But he always wants to kiss his dad good night.

Sometimes I get one of those perfect, wonderfully sincere "I love you, Dad" kisses. It's just a coincidence, I'm sure, but these are most common when I've just surprised him with a new toy or promised to buy him his very own pirate island in the Caribbean.

Sometimes he gives me a wet, silly fish-lips kiss. Sometimes it's brownie-flavored, if the remnants of his favorite late-night snack are still smeared all over his face.

Sometimes I'm the lucky recipient of what he calls a "movie-star kiss." That's when he grabs my head, crushes his mouth against mine, and holds me in a Hollywood-style lip-lock that lasts until *he* needs to come up for air, which can take up to five minutes.

And sometimes—usually when Mom has promised to read him the latest installment in a long-running, particularly exciting bedtime story—I get "chicken quickies." These are like the sanitary, speed-of-light pecks you give your mustachioed Aunt Mildred on Thanksgiving Day when she's standing there *waiting* and there's no escape.

Frankly, I love 'em all. Even when I'm left gasping for breath, groping for a washcloth, or feeling like somebody's Aunt Mildred. And if it were up to me, I'd still be getting good-night kisses from my son when he's a forty-two-year-old, six-foot-seven, 240-pound outlaw biker nicknamed "The Killer" by his former prison inmates.

By then, however, I probably won't have much say in the matter. By then, I'll be a slobbering geezer and my son will no doubt think he's too old or too cool or too masculine to do anything so little-boyish as kissing his father good night.

Oh, maybe I'll be able to manipulate him into the occasional "chicken quickie" when there's no one around, I'm *waiting,* and there's no escape. But fish-lip, brownie-flavored, and movie-star kisses, I fear, will be out of the question entirely. Unless he somehow evolves into such a pathetic weakling that I'll be able to remove my farina bib and unhook my heart-lung machine just long enough to overpower him.

At the rate this kid is growing, though, the safe money is on the "Killer" scenario. Instead of good-night kisses, I'll soon be getting firm handshakes. Or pats on the back. Or a speedy "See ya, Dad" as he bolts home to someone he's *not* too old or too cool or too masculine to kiss.

But you can bet the farm that, before he leaves, he'll plant one on his other. Otherwise, she'd overpower him. Even if his nickname is "The Killer."

If it seems like I'm doing an awful lot of advance worrying, well, the transition from kisses to handshakes has already begun. I walked my son to school the other day and made the mistake of trying to kiss him good-bye in front of his classmates.

"Daaaa-aaaad," he groaned, "I gotta go." And off he ran, surely wondering how he was going to explain his father's mortifying behavior to the guys on the playground.

Now, I happen to be an understanding parent. I wouldn't want a large, bearded man in a Hawaiian-print shirt kissing *me* in front of all my friends, either. But there are greater humiliations. Like when you're caught, red-handed, watching a "Three's Company" rerun on TV while appearing to be actually enjoying yourself. Or when reliable witnesses claim that you once considered buying a Yugo.

You know what I'm talking about. Things you could never live down. Things that could earn you the nickname "The Really Stupid Guy" instead of "The Killer." Things that, by comparison, make kissing your father seem perfectly respectable.

Ah, well. I'm willing to give and take. I'll settle for a firm handshake in the schoolyard. It's the good-night kisses I don't want to negotiate.

Last night, as I was putting my boy to bed, he gave me an "I love you, Dad" kiss *and* a movie-star kiss, both brownie-flavored. During the ensuing hug, I broke down and asked if he'd ever get too big to kiss me good night.

"Daaaa-aaaad," he groaned. "I'm your son. Sons always kiss their dads good night."

Hold that thought, Killer.

Dressed to Kill

My wife is psychic. She can always tell when I've dressed my kids. All she has to do is look at my son in his green dress shirt, blue swimming trunks, red-and-white gym socks, and black patent-leather shoes, and somehow, she just *knows* that I coordinated his outfit.

It's incredible. I keep expecting to open the silverware drawer and find that she's been practicing her Uri Geller routine on our spoons.

Then again, maybe I'm giving her sixth sense too much credit. After all, it wasn't until after a year of dating and about fifteen seconds of marriage that she realized I'm a full-time slob with absolutely no sense of style.

How this fact could have gone unnoticed by her for so long is a mystery. In every photograph that's ever been taken of me, my shirt is hanging halfway out of my trousers. This is a problem that's always plagued me. For a while I stopped tucking in my shirttails—and, like magic, they'd work themselves halfway *into* my trousers.

It's not that I haven't tried to improve in this area. Years ago a girlfriend (who noticed my fashion unconciousness immediately) informed me that one never mixes polka dots and stripes. Had she also told me that one can't mix polka dots with paisleys, plaids, or Hawaiian prints, the relationship might have lasted longer than it did. In time, she might have even agreed to be seen in public with me.

Another of my failings is that I can never find anything in my house. You can write down specific instructions, draw a map complete with directional arrows, focus a klieg light directly on the item in question, and I won't be able to find it.

**MICHAEL
BURKETT**
My wife knows this about me. Yet she continues to leave me notes like, "Bonzo's clothes are on top of his dresser," assuming:

1. I'm going to find the note.
2. I'm going to find the clothes.
3. I'm going to find Bonzo.

When I do find the note, I will not find the clothes. Or if I find the clothes, I will not find the note. And if I don't find the note, how do I know the clothes on his dresser (wherever that is) are the ones he's supposed to wear? Maybe they're dirty. I don't want to dress my son in dirty clothes. I'd rather he looked like me.

So traditionally, I will rummage through the dryer, looking for clean clothes and cursing my wife for not leaving me a note where I could find it (taped to my forehead, for example) and for not setting aside any clean clothes where I could find them (taped to my forehead, for example).

It can be said that I always find *something* for my kids to wear. One time I even had my daughter perfectly color-coordinated from neck to toe. I was so proud. She spent the whole day in those duds— cruising the mall with Dad, grabbing a Happy Meal at McDonald's, playing outside with all her toddler friends.

Then Mom came home and asked why in the world our little girl was in the front yard wearing her pajamas.

I honestly don't think I deserve all the blame for that incident. Even though my daughter is only eighteen months old, she's very bright. She could have asked me why I was taking her out of one pair of pajamas and putting her into another.

Or my wife could simply hide all my daughter's pajamas someplace I'd never find them—like the dresser drawer labeled "Your Daughter's Pajamas." But oooooh noooo. My wife just leaves me notes.

That's what she says, anyway. She could be lying. I've never actually found one.

Stop the Presses

Last week, I wouldn't have been caught dead with one of those "My-Child-Was-Named-Student-of-the-Month-at-Blah-Blah-Blah-Elementary-School" bumper stickers on my car. While parental pride is very nice, I believed, you've got to draw the line somewhere. And advertising your kids' scholastic achievements on the family station wagon seemed a good place to start.

Today, however, I'm a changed dad. You see, my son has been named Student of the Month. And there's a bumper sticker on my car to prove it.

Back in the sixties, there was a short-lived TV series called "The Guns of Will Sonnett," starring Walter Brennan as an Old West patriarch who rarely stopped praising the gunslinging abilities of his sons —and who concluded each of his monologues with, "No brag, just fact."

Clearly, these bumper stickers fall into the same category. Mikhail Gorbachev won the Nobel Peace Prize; no brag, just fact. Katharine Hepburn is a four-time Oscar winner; no brag, just fact. My son was named Student of the Month; no brag, just cold, hard, undeniable fact.

That's why I felt no shame as I adhered the bumper sticker to my car, phoned all our relatives with the big news, constructed a three-story float for the boy's gala victory parade, and mass-mailed the following press release.

Bonzo Burkett Aces Competition,
Sweeps "Student of Month" Honors

MESA, ARIZONA (AP)—In a stunning triumph that did not surprise his parents, boy wonder Bonzo Burkett, six, was elected Student of the Month at Freddy Krueger Elementary School, beating out millions of eligible youngsters nationwide. Including yours.

The unusually gifted first-grader was honored for "consistent improvement" in the areas of "maintaining a tidy work station, penmanship, punctuality, and finding his place in line during fire drills."

In addition to a handsome certificate, Bonzo also received a bumper sticker and a coupon for one free video rental. Asked how he would "spend" his prize, the budding genius replied, "Beats me. My dad glued *that* to our car, too."

The Freddy Krueger student body (aka "The Losers") learned of the election results from Bonzo's father, who ran through the school corridors screaming, "MY SON WAS NAMED STUDENT OF THE MONTH AND YOU WEREN'T! HA HA HA HA HA!"

The scene turned ugly when he was physically removed from the schoolgrounds by several third-grade crossing guards, whom the elder Burkett described as "the first of the petty, jealous 'little people' Bonzo's gonna forget the very *second* he becomes a staple celebrity on 'The New, New, NEW Hollywood Squares.'"

Within a few hours of the boy's landslide win, the state of Arizona had already begun to report enormous economic benefits.

"We've never seen anything like it," gushed a spokesperson for the Arizona Board of Tourism. "Bonzo's home has already replaced Graceland as the nation's most popular vacation destination, and no wonder. The tour is cheaper, the gift shops offer a wider variety of merchandise, and Bonzo isn't a dead fat guy."

Meanwhile, Bonzo's father admitted that while he is "very proud" of his son, "I remain deeply sympathetic toward all those less fortunate mothers and fathers—like you—who are doomed to spend all eternity bumper-stickerless.

"Therefore, I have very generously printed up seven million four-color, glow-in-the-dark bumper stickers which read, 'Michael Burkett's Child Was Named Student of the Month at Freddy Krueger Elementary School.' I'll be passing them out directly after the gala victory parade."

Now you know. The only thing more annoying than a proud parent with a bumper sticker is a proud parent with a newspaper column.

Who's the Boss?

Since there are more people outside the world's prisons than within them, I guess it's safe to assume that most child-rearing methods work, no matter how nutty they seem. But sometimes you wonder— like when you spend three days playing host to house guests from the What, Me Worry? School of Parenting.

Our visitors included one of my very best friends, who has remained one of my best friends since college. I have no qualms about discussing his cribside manner with unflinching candor because 1) ours is a friendship built on a firm bedrock of honesty, where praise and criticism have equal value, and 2) he is currently out of the country.

I hope.

You see, there are certain areas of honesty that can destroy the sturdiest of friendships, and this one tops the list. Even Ma Barker no doubt considered herself an excellent parent—and God help the well-intentioned, bigmouthed friend who insinuated anything to the contrary.

So just in case my pal *is* reading this, rest assured that I am referring to *another* old and valued friend, Bob of Zimbabwe.

Bob and his wife Bobbi (her real name) have a two-year-old son named Bobaloo (his real name, too) who may be the world's youngest head of household. It is Bobaloo who decides when it's time for Bobaloo to go to bed, what Bobaloo and everyone else in his family will eat, how much candy and cookies Bobaloo will consume between meals, and at what maddeningly slow pace Bob and Bobbi will live every aspect of their lives.

Bobaloo doesn't take naps (he doesn't like them) and doesn't drink milk (he prefers swigs of Dad's beer). He has no use for seat belts or other child restraining devices because they're uncomfortable (and, as his folks point out with incontestable accuracy, "They don't have 'em on buses"). Nor does Bobaloo like to walk all the way down the hall to the toilet, even though he's fully potty trained. (Diapers, the boy has discovered, are real playtime savers.)

In short, whatever Bobaloo wants, Bobaloo gets. When he yearns to toddle out the door and down the street all by himself, it's okay by his folks, who responded to my wife's politely understated shock by sighing, "I guess we're just not overprotective types." At restaurants, if it is Bobaloo's desire to knock over every filled glass on the table, that's fine, too. Bob and Bobbie just shrug as if to say, "Kids will be kids," then hand their son a bright, shiny steak knife in the hopes it will distract him long enough for everyone's lap to dry.

The ploy never works, but Bobaloo doesn't seem to mind. And really, what else matters?

The benefits of this approach are obvious. You get all the joys of parenting—and you skip the headaches. Why waste time arguing with a toddler when you can spend those same precious moments allowing his personality to develop, *au natural*, without grown-up restraints? Why risk the loss of his affection by making demands when you can elect him Family Emperor for Life? Why go to all the trouble of making and enforcing rules when he can make and enforce them for you?

Heck, within a few years, you could hand ALL your decisions over to the kid: Should I quit my job? Should we sell the house and join the circus? Should I undergo the triple by-pass surgery the doctor has recommended, or should we use the money for a lifetime supply of cake and ice cream?

What's right? What's wrong? *How should we live our lives?*

It would be like having an old-fashioned South Pacific volcano god right in your own home—which could be a lot of fun until Li'l Kahuna starts whining for a virgin sacrifice and you can't bring yourself to break with tradition by turning him down.

I have never claimed to be a perfect parent (modesty prohibits). But a wiser course of action, it seems, would be to prepare kids early on for the real, nasty, unfair world by saying "no" once every six months or so; to assume that most preschoolers aren't ready to run their own lives; and to accept the fact that no matter how accommodating a parent you are, there will be a period of years when your children will harbor no doubt that you are a complete twit.

Of course, I could be wrong. Maybe I should sit down with my kids over brewskies and steak knives and ask *them*. If they'll let me.

Phonus Interruptus

Kids can't help it. It's a Pavlovian thing, set off by the ringing of a telephone. At that moment, they are compelled by mysterious, unseen forces to ask you really dumb questions for the duration of the call.

You can say, "Please, sweetheart, can't you see I'm on the phone?" You can say, "Don't interrupt, my love, it's Ed McMahon calling long distance with good news from Publisher's Clearinghouse." You can say, "PIPE DOWN OR YOUR BELOVED HAMSTER FLUFFY GOES STRAIGHT BACK TO THE PET STORE!" It just doesn't make any difference. The child will continue to rattle on until you or the caller hangs up in a huff. (Or a minute and a huff, as Groucho Marx would say.)

The typical scenario goes like this:

Riiiiing!

"Hello? . . . oh, hi, Mr. McMahon! What a pleasant surprise!—"

"Dad? Dad? Dad? Dad? Dad? Dad? Dad? Dad? Dad? Dad?"

"Please, sweetheart, can't you see I'm on the telephone?"

"But Dad? But Dad? But Dad? But Dad? But Dad?"

"Don't interrupt, my love, it's Ed McMahon calling long distance with good news from Publisher's Clearinghouse."

"But Dad, it's very, very, very, very, very, very important."

"I'm sorry, Mr. McMahon. Will you excuse me for a minute? Thank you . . . ALL RIGHT! MAKE IT QUICK! WHAT DO YOU WANT?"

"It's very important, Dad."

"I KNOW! YOU'VE SAID THAT! WHAT DO YOU WANT?"

"Dad? Dad? Dad? Dad? Dad? Are all ducks green or just *some* ducks?"

"JUST *SOME* DUCKS! NOW GO PLAY IN YOUR ROOM AND LOCK THE DOOR AND DON'T COME OUT UNTIL I SAY SO!"

"Okay. Thanks, Dad."

"Sorry for the interruption, Mr. McMahon, but—"

"Dad? Dad? Dad? Dad? Dad? Dad? Dad? Dad? Dad? Dad?"

Obviously, this is where even the most mild-mannered adults start screaming, "PIPE DOWN OR YOUR BELOVED HAMSTER FLUFFY GOES STRAIGHT BACK TO THE PET STORE!" (In homes where the child doesn't own a hamster, that threat is usually altered to something like, "Pipe down or I'll go out, buy a hamster, bring it home, name it Fluffy, wait until you bond with the thing and then take it straight back to the pet store!" But that never works, either.)

The only times kids don't interrupt the telephone conversations of their parents are 1) during family vacations to impoverished foreign countries where there are no phones, 2) when they are making so much noise that they temporarily deafen themselves and cannot hear the phone ringing, 3) when the caller is a fellow parent who might actually understand your problem, and 4) when the person on the other end of the line is one of those cretins who calls for no apparent reason to gab for hours on a variety of subjects neither of you cares about.

In the latter case, I have been known to put my hand over the mouthpiece and *beg* my kids to interrupt. But no. They always have better things to do—until the next call, anyway.

What many people do not realize about children is that their aural senses are so acute they can hear telephones that are ringing miles away. This explains why they also start jabbering whenever you go to the bathroom, pick up a newspaper, or attempt to complete the kinds of urgent conversations which begin with your spouse saying, "Oh, by the way, the police came by the house looking for you this afternoon because..."

"Dad? Dad? Dad? Dad? Dad? Dad? Dad? Dad? Dad? Dad?"

I still don't know what the police wanted. Threatening hamsters is legal in America. I'm almost certain of it.

Worry Wart

It has been scientifically proven that raising children kills brain cells, so I may be suffering from severe memory loss. The way I remember it, though, one of the nicest things about being a kid was that there wasn't much to worry about.

The few concerns I had as a child were the king-sized, doomsday-type drummed into me by adults: a Communist takeover...nuclear war...the inescapable fact that my home town on the coast of northern California would one day be hit by such a monster earthquake it would sink to the bottom of the Pacific, and those of us who couldn't body-surf to safety would be eaten alive by eels.

Today, I can look back and laugh at those worries—except the one about the earthquake, which came true. Good thing I come from a family of accomplished body-surfers.

I bring this up because my son frets over *everything*. Perhaps its a natural by-product of growing up in an age defined by ecological disaster, social unrest, crime, senseless violence, and candy that's scientifically designed to look like snot. But there's not a molehill in creation that he can't turn into the Himalayan Mountains.

During automobile trips of any duration, he doesn't just worry that we'll run out of gas. He worries that we'll be stranded roadside on some desolate, godforsaken stretch of highway until we die of starvation or exposure, at which point our bodies will be dragged off by wild animals and fed to their young, who will scatter our skeletal remains all over the countryside so no one will ever be able to find us.

This kid approaches new experiences much like a hypochondriac would approach the community toothbrush in a leper colony. Take him to an amusement park and ask if he'd like to ride the roller coaster, he will at first answer in the affirmative. But the shorter the line gets, the more he will consider the "What ifs."

"What if it goes too fast and flies off the track? What if it soars through the air and crashes into a building? What if the building explodes and starts a big fire and all the firemen in the world can't put it out? What if..."

By the time it's our turn to board the thing, he's begging for dear life.

Nothing, however, worries my son more than *change*. Several times this past summer I found him sitting on the living room sofa, pretending to watch TV, quietly fighting back tears.

"What's wrong, honey?"

"I...I don't want to start second grade."

"Why?"

"I'm afraid."

"Afraid of what? It won't be very different from first grade."

"Yes it will. I won't be in the same class with my friends and all the new kids won't like me and the teacher will be mean and I don't know where the lunchboxes are supposed to go and..."

To him, second grade was a fate worse than being eaten alive by eels, and no matter what my wife or I said, he wanted no part of it. Not until two days before school started, anyway, when he received a personal letter from his new teacher—a woman who has clearly dealt with nervous, would-be grade-school dropouts before.

In introducing herself, she mentioned that her husband was a policeman, which my son thought was definitely awesome. Even better, she also said that one of her own kids owned a California king snake, and promised to bring it to school!

That changed everything. Now the lad couldn't *wait* to become a second-grader. And when the Big Morning arrived, his only worry was that his hair might not be perfectly combed. (Obviously, he wanted to make a good impression on the snake.)

Well, the teacher did indeed bring the reptile to class, and my son was the first kid allowed to hold it. He was still jabbering about the experience at bedtime; about how the snake felt, how big it was, how he was sure he'd seen its fangs.

A few hours later, I went back to his room to check on him. After being struck anew by the sweet vulnerability of a sleeping child (a nightly ritual of all parents), the awful thought came to me. "What if the snake had bitten him? What if it had coiled itself around his neck? What if it mistook his hand for a rat? What if...?"

Maybe second grade isn't a fate worse than being eaten alive by eels. But it's close.

Gender Mercies

In order to be a topflight journalist like myself, you need keen powers of observation to pick up on the subtleties of life that escape the common folk. And lately, one thing I've been noticing is that the difference between fathers and mothers is as great as the difference between men and women.

Really. Trust me. I'm a trained professional journalist.

To wit:

Mothers dress their children as if every day were Sunday. Fathers dress their children as if every day were Saturday—and since they're not planning to be seen by anyone they know, what the heck, Friday's clothes don't look all that dirty.

When mothers prepare dinner, they draw from the four basic food groups. When fathers prepare dinner, they draw from the four Tupperware containers closest to the refrigerator door.

Mothers take their children to the state fair to see the 4-H exhibits. Fathers take their children to the state fair to impress them with their manly ability to spend ninety-three dollars trying to knock down enough aluminum milk bottles to win a four-inch stuffed animal of indeterminate species that nobody wants.

A mother will go to the store for bread and milk, and return with enough groceries to feed Bangladesh for a year. A father will go to the store for bread and milk and return with bread, nacho-flavored Doritos, and five dollars' worth of lottery tickets.

A mother will recoil in horror at the sight of the family dog sliming her baby with saliva. A father will delight in this bonding ritual between a boy and his dog, and try to calm the mother by pointing out that canine saliva is among the most sanitary substances known to modern science. Or that's what he heard. Somewhere.

A mother will buy her youngster an ice cream cone as a reward for good behavior. A father will buy one upon being suckered by the screaming brat's promise that he'll start being good as soon as somebody buys him an ice cream cone.

Mothers don't make any major purchases unless the box says "Assembly Required." Fathers don't buy anything that comes in a box in the off-chance that assembly will be required.

Mothers sometimes give their kids between-meal snacks. Fathers sometimes give their kids between-snack meals.

Mothers wash dishes after every meal. Fathers wash dishes when the sink is so full you have to go to the bathroom for a glass of water.

A mother will say "no" and mean it. A father will say "no" and mean it until the mother corrects him.

After a mother has bathed her children, the bathroom will appear untouched. After a father has bathed his children, only the soap, washcloth, and shampoo will appear untouched.

Mothers want their sons to be sensitive, caring human beings. Fathers want their sons to be sensitive, caring human beings who know how to maim or seriously injure a 340-pound enemy quarterback without getting bounced from the game or earning a penalty.

Mothers think of their daughter's first date as a rite of passage. Fathers think of their daughter's first date as a virgin sacrifice.

When their children leave home, mothers worry that they won't eat right. Fathers worry that they'll be back in an hour, eating right out of the fridge and asking for another loan.

A father hopes and prays his grown children will remember everything he taught them. A mother hopes and prays her grown children will remember they have parents.

Nicotine Fit

It's easy for adults to rationalize their most idiotic weaknesses in the company of other adults. Throw a kid into the picture, however, and the process becomes damn near impossible.

"What did you do in school today?" I asked my son, expecting to get the usual lowdown on the subtraction problem of the week or the construction-paper volcano he made and decorated with teensy charred corpses.

"We talked about drugs," the boy answered. "I learned that drugs are very, very bad. People who use them die and go to jail."

"Well, yes, they can," I agreed. "But not necessarily in that order."

"My teacher asked if we knew anyone who used drugs. I said, 'Yeah. My dad.' "

"WHAT!?!?!"

"My teacher says cigarettes are drugs, and you smoke cigarettes. Are you gonna die and go to jail?"

"Honey, people only go to prison for using drugs that are against the law. Those are *bad* drugs. But there are also good drugs, like the medicine a doctor gives you when you're sick."

"Are cigarettes good drugs?"

"Well, ahhhh, no . . ."

"Dad, why do you smoke cigarettes?"

Geez, I thought. Why couldn't he interrogate me about something *simple*, like the birds and the bees, the meaning of life, or the popularity of the TV show "Studs"?

It's not like I don't have a swell excuse for turning my lungs into twin scale models of the La Brea tar pits. You see, my ever-dwindling supply of brain cells simply refuses to work until they're slathered in nicotine. Every time I've tried to quit smoking, I'd succeed until I found myself staring at a killer deadline—at which point my most creative thought is, *I need a cigarette!* Not exactly Pulitzer Prize–worthy material.

This preoccupation lasts until the deadline draws closer and I have no choice but to 1) light up, or 2) get a job that doesn't require functioning gray matter, like those fast-food cashiers who ask if you want french fries with your pancakes.

To my slight credit, I don't smoke at home. And I'm way too smart to pollute my bodily temple with Camels or Marlboros or any of those brands guaranteed to increase one's masculinity, testosterone level, and desire to wear a cowboy hat. No, I smoke "ultra-lite" cigarettes—and frankly, it's comforting to know that if I get lung cancer or heart disease, it will be of the ultra-lite variety, requiring only ultra-lite chemotherapy and ultra-lite heart-bypass surgery.

Another reason it's been easy to live with my addiction is that, despite the current social status of smokers (who are ranked directly between French-kissing lepers and newspaper editors), it is still possible to find a sympathetic ear in the adult world.

But nowadays, I was discovering, a smoker would have to hang out with a grade-school junkie street gang to get any slack from a kid.

"Dad? Why do you like cigarettes?"

"It's not that I like them, son. It's just that, well, once you start smoking, it's not easy to stop."

"That's what my teacher says about bad drugs."

"Well, she's right, but ..."

Apparently, the boy sensed that our conversation was going nowhere fast, because he ended it much like the Indians at Little Big Horn ended George Custer's retirement plans.

"Dad, cigarettes are stupid. Smokers are stupid. You're gonna die and go to jail."

My son wasn't entirely correct, of course. But he was right enough to make me retreat to a designated smoking area, inhale some ultra-lite carbon monoxide, and render myself capable of re-rationalization.

I know many adults who'd understand. It's those buttinski second-graders you've got to watch out for.

Holiday in Whoville

On the second of March, in the Jungle of Snoo,
Or at least thereabouts, he was born, it is true.
The world was a much different place way back then;
Those years before Dr. Seuss picked up a pen.

There weren't Juggling Jotts, not one Zinn-a-Zu,
And no random Yertles or Befts or Jibboo.
Naturally, too, there was nary a Natch
(Those cave-dwelling beasties no hunter can catch).

No Mulligawtanies, fast as the wind,
From the blistering sands of the Desert of Zind.
No gussets, no gooches, no New McGrew Zoo,
No sneetches or Greetches, no minuscule Who.

In those dull, dreary days was the desperate need
For something *alive* for children to read.
They'd all had their fill of Dick, Jane, and Spot,
Running and jumping—for what? All for naught.

Few kids knew then that words can excite
In fantastic explosions of color and light.
That was the quandary Seuss sought to fix,
And he did, throwing whimsey and wit in the mix.

MICHAEL BURKETT

Thanks to Seuss, and to Horton, we learned, after all,
That a person's a person, no. matter how small;
And that egg-sitting elephants could hatch—how absurd!—
History's very first pachyderm bird!

We ate green eggs and ham with the Cat in the Hat
(But no, Sam-I-Am, we don't like them with gnat).
And the Circus McGurkus! Where a walrus named Rolf
Did marvelous tricks (if Seuss said so hissolf).

It wasn't just youngsters Doc Seuss did enthrall;
Parents themselves had a tongue-twisting ball
Putting their offspring to bed with such chums
As fluff-muffled Truffles and Drum-Tummied Snumms.

196

And now those wee tykes, who've left home and grown,
Are knotting their tongues for kids all their own,
Who'll one day grow up and produce even more
Seuss fans by the gross and the ton and the score.

Some Grinches gripe, "Seuss is much too unblandish!
His stories pure nonsense, his drawings outlandish!
He puts words together without moral or thought!"
But those folks all missed what their children have caught . . .

Like the poor Humming-Fish, who no longer hummed
'Cause their pond was polluted and their gills were all gummed.
Or the Yooks who battled and bombed a Zook town
'Cause the Zooks ate their bread with the butter side down.

So forget the few ranters, they cynical ravers,
And proceed to assemble the Poogle-horn players!

It's the good doctor's birthday! A fine time to cheer
The wonder and wisdom he spreads every year.

When will he stop? The man's eighty-seven!
(In Bingle-Bug years, that's two-thousand eleven!)
Only one thing's for sure, and it's worth more than gold:
A wizard's a wizard, no matter how old.

■ ■ ■

The party had not yet begun to subside
When the news was announced that the wizard had died.
But, truth be known, he'll remain on the loose
As long as kids say, "Dad, read Dr. Seuss!"

Daddy Dearest

Last night, two friends dropped by with their fourteen-month-old daughter. Wherever Daddy went, baby followed. Whenever Daddy sat down, baby begged to sit in his lap. Whenever anyone else tried to touch the child—including her own mother—she'd feign sudden respiratory failure until Daddy came to the rescue. Then the kid would gurgle and coo and make all those happy noises normal toddlers make only when they're starring in diaper commercials.

Frankly, this blatant display of father-worship irritated the hell out of me. You'd have felt the same way if you had sired a—yes, I'm going to say it—a *MOMMY'S GIRL*.

I was forced to accept this painful truth about six months ago—the very morning my daughter learned how to run and scream at the same time. I was trying to kick-start my brain with newsprint and caffeine when she tramped into the kitchen, caught her first morning's sight of Dear Old Dad, and bolted in the opposite direction while wailing, "GO AWAY! I DON'T WANT YOU! I WANT MOMMY!"

I tried not to take it personally. But it isn't easy being on the receiving end of a loved one's total, absolute rejection. Especially when you're too groggy to notice that you've not only poured yourself a bowl of Sugar-Fortified Cocoa-Honey-Marshmallow Grahams, you're actually eating them.

And it didn't help when my daughter would return in her mother's arms, bestowing upon her the first kisses and hugs of the day. Affection that rightfully belonged to me.

The good news is that our second-born has matured to the point where she no longer becomes suicidal at the mere sight of me. Now she runs straight to Mom without saying a word.

You'd think I'd be used to this treatment by now. When my son was two, he didn't want anything to do with me either. And his attitude hasn't changed much since then.

Not long ago, the boy scraped his knee and worked himself into such hysteria that if my eyesight were any worse, I'd have assumed his leg had been ripped off at the hip. But as soon as he noticed that I was the sole parent on duty, his panic subsided.

"Uh, where's Mom?" he asked. I explained that she was at work and wouldn't be home for a few hours. "Oh," he said, heading back outside. "Never mind."

My own son doesn't trust me! What did he think I was gonna do? Look at his wound and say, "Uh-oh! We'd better pour some Liquid Plumber on that! But first, let's *really* make it bleed! Maybe if I whack it with this hammer a few times..."

At least my kids are consistent. In all matters of discussion, it is automatically assumed that Father Knows Nothing. If I tell my son, "No, you may not climb into the microwave oven and pretend it's the cockpit of the Starship *Enterprise*," he will immediately check with Mom for a *reliable* ruling.

It makes no sense. I'm the household authority figure who always wrestles with these kids until we break something. I'm the one who lets them watch almost any TV show they want until Mom pulls up in the driveway. I'm the one who thinks Eskimo Pies and Oreos add up to a fine, well-rounded meal. If it weren't for me, the little ingrates wouldn't have a life!

So why am I their second-favorite parent? There are five possible explanations:

1. My wife is secretly paying our children to like her more than me.

2.   My wife is an evil hypnotist who has taken control of their minds and brainwashed them into thinking I'm a big, know-nothing, chuckle-headed jerk.

3.   I *am* a big, know-nothing, chuckle-headed jerk (an absurd notion that would be vehemently denied by anyone who knows me).

4.   Children are lousy judges of character (which would explain why they are not allowed to vote, marry, or hang out in singles' bars).

5.   Women have some kind of weird, inexplicable, God-given magical power over their offspring.

That last theory sounded pretty solid until we were visited by our pals and their dad-addicted daughter. Now I'm leaning toward the evil-hypnotist idea.

My wife has her own opinion, of course. I'm not about to repeat it here, but suffice to say it's an absurd notion that would be vehemently denied by anyone who knows me. Not counting the members of my immediate family.

Ready! Aim! Stomp!

It's a tragic sight, and it's taking place in living rooms all across America: sweet, innocent children transformed into rampaging, brain-drained electro-zombies, insatiable in their lust for death and destruction.

I have seen the horror. My son has discovered Super Nintendo.

We tried to save him. We had vowed to never allow a home video game system into our home. We'd seen what they'd done to his best friend, Brian; once an abnormally normal kid, now an abnormally short and glassy-eyed sofa spud whose last conversation with his parents —on April 9, 1991—consisted of the words, "Accessories. I must have accessories."

For the uninitiated (ha ha), Super Nintendo was designed specifically for parents who fear their children aren't spending nearly enough time blobbing out in front of the television set, or entirely too much time interacting with other human beings. For families on the move, there's a battery-operated, hand-held version called Game Boy which permits children to be antisocial wherever they go.

Although hundreds of different game cartridges are available for purchase by the filthy rich, it is impossible for any adult to tell them apart. Whether the name of the game is "Billy Bunny's Birthday Surprise" or "Festering Astro-Mutant Flesh-Eaters from the Planet Vomitus," the message remains the same: that life's greatest rewards await those who most effectively destroy everything in sight before they themselves are bombed, blasted, bazookaed, strafed, squashed, or scorched to death.

My son was introduced to the joys of Super Nintendo during a visit to the coast of Maine, of all places. I'd been warned that our vacation cottage was equipped with the Evil Machine, but I wasn't worried. We were smack dab in one of Mother Nature's finest amusement parks, where there are countless attractions to lure a boy outside and keep him there.

The first of this great state's features to be noticed by my son was the mosquitoes. I tried to tell him that every wonderland has its price. In Disneyland, I said, you've got long lines; at Sea World you risk getting soaked by stunt-whales; and on the coast of Maine you can be turned into take-home food by flying squadrons of disease-carrying vermin the size of Mothra.

After that speech, my son made only one voluntary move toward the front door—and that was to nudge his little sister outside in hopes of witnessing his first, real-life feeding frenzy. You can imagine his disappointment when she adopted the mosquitoes as pets and started giving them names like "Kermit" and "Big Bird."

Adamant in his refusal to venture outside, bored out of his skull and determined to wreak havoc on *something*, the boy turned to Super Nintendo. And we didn't stop him. We'd only be there for three weeks. What could it hurt?

His game of choice was "Super Mario World," in which players assume the roles of two cute cartoon handymen named Mario and Luigi. Their happy mission—and yours, should you choose to accept it—is to stomp the life out of every cute cartoon creature they encounter while attempting to rescue a cute cartoon princess-in-distress. She is the sole inhabitant of "Super Mario World" you're not supposed to destroy, but most kids get so caught up in their marathon video killing spree they try to stomp the life out of her, too.

Thirty minutes into my son's first game, I understood why this brand of "home entertainment" inspires such bloodlust. It's the tinny, maddeningly repetitive music that plays nonstop and grates on your nerves to the point that, even when you're four rooms away, you want to climb to the top of the nearest belltower and start sniping at passers-by on the off-chance you'll plug the Nintendo employee who's responsible.

Three weeks into my son's first game, my wife wrestled me to the ground, confiscated my rifle, and comforted me with the news that our vacation was over and I'd never have to listen to that music again.

She may have saved hundreds of lives, including mine and that of one very lucky Nintendo employee. But our son was lost. All he could say during the three thousand–mile trip home was, "Game Boy. I must have Game Boy. And, of course, the accessories."

Small Blessings

Last Thanksgiving, as countless relatives gathered in our dining room, my son was elected to deliver the mealtime prayer. On such short notice, this was the best he could come up with:

"Dear God. Thank you for the food we eat, and for . . . um, the food we eat. And thank you for . . . ahhhh, the food we eat. Amen."

Now there's a kid who knows what Thanksgiving is all about.

This year, we've actually given the boy some time to prepare and rehearse his list. So far, he says, it includes the food we eat (still in the Number One slot); his family; his best friend, Brian; his six-year-old fiancée, Stephanie; the entire line of spin-off merchandising inspired by *The Teenage Mutant Ninja Turtles;* and our new neighbor, Jimmy.

If that last entry doesn't rip out your heart and stomp on it, you haven't met Jimmy.

Forty-two years ago, at the age of three, Jimmy was hit in the head by a flying baseball bat. According to the story I've been told, his parents (now dead) were too poor to take him to the hospital and too religious to think he would not recover on his own.

The reason Jimmy stopped talking entirely, they believed, was that he was angry at them for somehow allowing the accident to happen. Not until two years later, when they tried to enroll him in school, was their son diagnosed as severely brain-damaged.

Jimmy spent the next few decades in various state-funded institutions where, in the fifties and sixties, the term "health care" often meant uninterrupted physical, emotional, and sexual abuse. He did begin to build a vocabulary during this period, however . . . and when he joined my son and me on a recent afternoon walk, we heard a few of the words he'd picked up.

Pointing to a house, I asked, "Hey, Jimmy. What's that?" He said, "A boy." I pointed to a car. He said, "A flower." I pointed to a row of bushes. He said, "Switches."

Switches?

"To beat Jimmy."

That's his one and only reliable memory. Ask him to tell you his mother's name, he might answer Henry (his father), Helen (his sister), Mark (his brother), Twinkie (his cat), or, occasionally, Betty (his mother). But he never forgets the source and purpose of those switches.

Today, Jimmy lives with loving relatives who can't tell if he'll ever be able to distinguish a boy from a house, alligators from rocks, a shoe from the color yellow, or even laughter from tears. As far as they know, Jimmy has never expressed a recognizable human emotion.

At least, not until the other day, when Jimmy was being led home and, without prompting, called out to my son, "See ya, pal."

Now, compared to the parting of the Red Sea, the breaking of bread to feed the multitudes, or the image of the Virgin Mary appearing on a garage door in Elgin, Illinois, this was not a *huge* miracle, I suppose. But "Pal" is a word no one had ever heard Jimmy use. A word with a very definite emotional connection.

Yes, I know. It's possible Jimmy has no idea what "pal" means. But maybe he does.

It's possible he'll never say it again. But maybe he will.

It's possible that, tomorrow morning, Jimmy won't even recognize my son. But I hope he does.

That is what Jimmy has given me. After a lifetime of looking skyward for big miracles, winning lottery tickets, and the meaning of life, along comes this bat-battered forty-five-year-old-man with something truly worthy of a six-year-old's Thanksgiving prayer: a few slivers of hope that could vanish by morning, like a garage-door Virgin Mary.

But then again, maybe they won't.

As the Fur Flies

It must spring from genetic memory; a few random brain waves inherited from our prehistoric ancestors who viewed animals strictly as food, fur coats, or threats. Maybe that's why my two-year-old daughter seems so determined to kill our new kitten.

I don't think that's her actual intent. She loves this feline. A lot. That's why she can't walk from one room to another without picking it up by the head or the neck or the ears or the whiskers. (It can now be said with absolute certainty that, in our home, there is indeed ample room to swing a cat.)

Sadly, this is not a mutual admiration society. Whenever the kitten sees my daughter toddling his way, he howls, runs, and disappears for days at a time. To my little girl, this is a fun game akin to hide-and-seek. To the cat, I suspect, it's more like a Godzilla movie in which he's been forced to play the role of a Tokyo pedestrian.

It was my wife's idea to get a cat, and she could not be dissuaded even when I reminded her of the last one we owned—a bulimic, psychotic beast we named "Audrey" after the insatiable flesh-eating Venus flytrap from outer space in the movie *Little Shop of Horrors*. The one that constantly bellowed "Feed me! Feed me!"

Audrey was one of a few dozen kittens to catch my wife's eye as we strolled past a pet store window. We were newlyweds at the time, so when she begged to take one home, I could hardly turn her down. This kind of generosity lasts well into the third or fourth week of marriage.

"Go ahead," I answered. "Which one do you want?"

"*You* choose," she said sweetly.

I assumed my wife was leaving the selection up to me because I was the man of the house and would therefore make the wisest decision. In reality, she was thinking that if my cat of choice turned out to be, oh, bulimic or psychotic or all of the above, she could turn to me every thirty seconds or so for the rest of the creature's natural life and say, "Don't blame me. *You* picked her out."

This kind of generosity lasts well into the third or fourth eon of marriage.

Although Audrey has been in kitty heaven about four years now, and although I celebrate the anniversary of her demise as enthusiastically as anyone in my family (who do you think shells out for the Roman candles and champagne?), I am still blamed for her reign of terror in our household.

"Maybe we shouldn't let Dad help us find a new cat," my son said to his mother as they were plotting their search. "After all, he picked out *Audrey.*"

I cannot begin to describe the overwhelming sense of joy that came over me upon being voted out of this family project. The only thing that could have made me happier was if they'd brought home a cat that was even loopier than Audrey.

Well, wouldn't you know it, the eight-week-old furball they adopted was as cute and cuddly and lovable and nonbulimic as domesticated critters come. My son named him "Sherlock Holmes" for his unrelenting curiosity. And none of us could keep our hands off him—including my daughter, who has yet to note the difference between dolls (which have removeable heads and limbs) and cats (which don't).

The main reason my wife wanted a cat, of course, was so we could thrill to the sight of our little girl bonding with her first pet. And that's exactly what we'd be doing if we weren't so busy running after the kid, screaming, "DON'T TOUCH THE CAT! YOU'RE GONNA KILL THE CAT! DROP THE CAT! DON'T ... TOUCH ... THE ... CAT!!!!!"

In the long run, though, things have turned out nicely. As we chase my daughter around the house, begging for poor Sherlock's life, I turn to my wife every thirty seconds or so and say, "Don't blame me. *You* gave birth to her."

Field and Scream

A large, bearded man. A small, unbearded boy. A weekend in the wilderness.

This is their diary.

Day One

3:36 P.M.: We arrive at our campsite. Bonzo thinks he sees a wolf and refuses to get out of the car.

4:13 P.M.: I realize that the six-person, three-room tent I purchased for this little outing requires six people, power tools, and a building permit to assemble. I ask Bonzo for help. He thinks he sees a vampire bat and refuses to get out of the car.

6:28 P.M.: Thanks to a passing construction crew, our tent is up. To show my gratitude, I sublet one of the rooms to them at a bargain rate.

7:14 P.M.: Dinnertime! I carve points on a couple of long twigs to roast hot dogs over the open campfire. When my hot dog catches fire, Bonzo decides that this looks like fun and finally gets out of the car.

8:22 P.M.: After incinerating an entire package of franks, Bonzo becomes hungry and asks what we're having for dinner.

8:38 P.M.: Bonzo asks for ketchup on his raw hot dog.

8:49 P.M.: Darkness falls. Bonzo wants to sit by the campfire and tell ghost stories. I make up one about mutant, bloodthirsty trees that sneak up on campers in the middle of the night and eat them, sleeping bags and all.

8:53 P.M.: Bonzo refuses to get out of the car.

10:32 P.M.: At last! Bonzo is asleep. I'd be asleep, too, if it weren't for this damned stick shift.

11:48 P.M.: I carry Bonzo to the tent and pray he doesn't wake up until daybreak.

Day Two

6:04 A.M.: Bonzo awakes. He has to go Number One and asks me to take him to the campground bathroom, which is approximately one mile away. I explain that, in this situation, it is acceptable to step outside and relieve oneself on a tree.

6:05 A.M.: "Next time," I tell Bonzo, "find a tree that is more than two inches away from the tent . . . on a *downhill* slope."

6:08 A.M.: We move the tent to a dry spot.

7:33 A.M.: Breakfast! I cook up a hearty campfire meal of bacon, eggs, and campfire ash. Bonzo looks at his plate and says, "Dad, I'll eat this if you really want me to." Clearly, he's lying.

7:46 A.M.: Bonzo asks for ketchup on his raw hot dog.

8:08 A.M.: We go fishing. Bonzo is excited.

8:14 A.M.: We haven't caught anything. Bonzo is bored.

8:17 A.M.: Bonzo mistakes his fishing pole for a laser sword and some passing hikers for the Imperial Army. We return to camp.

8:52 A.M.: Bonzo is so bored he wants to go fishing again. But I have a better idea. We take a nap.

12:14 P.M.: Lunchtime! I cook up a hearty campfire meal of corned beef hash and something that appears to have fallen from a tree. It looks dead, but we're not certain.

12:20 P.M.: I ask for ketchup on my raw hot dog.

12:53 P.M.: Bonzo is still so bored he wants to go fishing again. Against my better judgment, we go fishing. Bonzo is excited.

2:15 P.M.: BONZO CATCHES HIS VERY FIRST FISH! I have never seen my son so happy.

2:17 P.M.: The fish is dead. I have never seen my son so sad. He had already named his catch "Spike," thinking we were going to take it home to live in our aquarium.

2:18 P.M.: I explain the food chain to Bonzo. He calls me a fish murderer.

2:19 P.M.: We return to camp. Bonzo remains inconsolable until I take out a large hunting knife, cut the head off his fish, and yank out its innards. "Wow!" he exclaims, "That's neat! Can I pull out some of its guts, too?" I have never seen my son so happy. Now he says he's *glad* I'm a fish murderer—and since we've got the knife out, could we murder something else?

6:12 P.M.: Dinnertime! I cook up a hearty campfire meal of blackened trout. Bonzo takes one bite and asks for ketchup on his raw hot dog.

6:43 P.M.: Bonzo wants to take the fish bones to school for show and tell. I think that's cute until he also asks to take the head and guts.

7:10 P.M.: Bonzo says he can't wait for it to get dark so we can sit by the campfire and tell more ghost stories. I laugh and make a mental note to have the boy committed to an insane asylum as soon as we return home.

9:45 P.M.: We go to bed. In the tent. Before he falls asleep, Bonzo tells me what a wonderful day he had. I change my mind about the insane asylum.

Day Three

7:35 A.M.: Breakfast! We don't take any chances. We head straight for the raw hot dogs and ketchup.

8:18 A.M.: I tell Bonzo it's time to start packing for the long trip home. He refuses to get out of the tent. I change my mind about the insane asylum.

The Big Sleep

My son has known for some time that bugs die when you step on them, dogs and cats die when they get hit by cars, and goldfish die for no apparent reason. But it has remained his firm conviction that human death is no more than a Hollywood plot device used when the bad guys need more than a sound thrashing to straighten them out.

I never went out of my way to correct this impression. This is, after all, a seven-year-old whose biggest worry in July is what he'll be getting for Christmas. The subject was hard to avoid, though, when out of the blue, during a milk-and-bread run, the boy said, "Dad, are you and Mom ever going to die?"

A parent's natural response in the face of a question like that is to conjure up a big, fat, happy lie—partly because it's the easy way out, and partly because a child's concept of time doesn't even *begin* to develop until he's old enough to read the program listings in *TV Guide*. Answer "yes" or any variation thereof to The Death Question, and he will fully expect you to expire on the spot.

Even unflinchingly honest moms and dads have been known to sidestep the issue with jolly sentiments like, "Well, you know, life is so wonderful we should enjoy it while we can and, say, what do you suppose Santa will be bringing you for Christmas this year?"

Of course, the problem with this approach is that, unless your child is dumber than a box of rocks, he will see through your pitiably thin smokescreen, divine the truth, give up on you as a source of reliable information, and fully expect you to expire on the spot.

In short, there is no escape.

"Yes, son, your mother and I will die someday," I said, ever-so-blithely, quickly adding, "but not for a very, *very* long time. So it's not something we need to think about now."

When the kid started bawling, I cursed myself for not taking the big-fat-happy-lie route.

"You mean . . . MOM IS GONNA DIE?!?!?"

Normally, I would have been hurt by such a snub. In this case, however, it was a relief to know I'd only be consoling the boy over the prospect of losing *one* parent.

"Honey, it won't happen for a long time," I said, choosing to make the truth as upbeat and uncomplicated as possible. "People don't die until they're very old."

"Dad, you're old now."

You're pushing it, kid.

"Yes, I know. But I'm not *very* old. Yet."

"So . . . does everybody die?"

"Someday, yes."

"You mean . . . Grandma and Grandpa are gonna die? And Uncle Bill? And my sister? And Stephanie and Brian and Miss Patterson and all my friends . . ."

"Honey, not for a long time . . ."

"AND ME? . . . I'M GONNA DIE, TOO?!?!?"

"Ahhh . . ."

"DADDY! I DON'T WANNA DIE! I DON'T WANNA DIE! IT'S NOT FAIR!!"

Jeez. And the day had started so nicely, too.

"Sweetheart, what I'm talking about is soooo far into the future there really is no reason to worry about it. You have your *whole life* ahead of you. You're going to do all sorts of neat, exciting things.

You'll grow up, maybe get married, have kids of your own, travel the world, do anything you want..."

The boy was starting to cheer up. "I could even watch 'Toxic Avenger' on TV?"

"Absolutely," I said, thinking it must have been a conversation like this that spawned the phrase "over my dead body."

"And you and Mom won't die for a very, *very* long time?"

"Not for a very, very long time."

Once we arrived at the supermarket and my son caught sight of the toy aisle, the subject—thank heavens—was dropped. But not for long. A few days later, my wife had to throw the kids into the car and rush me to the hospital because of a sudden, immobilizing attack of abdominal pain.

As my son watched total strangers wheel me down the emergency-ward halls to some scary, mysterious hospital nowhereland, he turned to his mother and spoke for the first time since we'd left the house.

"Dad lied," he said.

Things Change

It's stunning how quickly life changes the second you're admitted into an emergency ward for seven hours of abdominal surgery followed by a three-and-a-half week hospital stay.

Everything changes. Your worries. Your priorities. Your acceptance of ice chips and Jello-O as a satisfying, full-course meal. The importance of one day meeting your grandchildren. The importance of one day meeting your great-grandchildren. Your appreciation of the technological genius it required to design an electronically controlled bed that, at the push of an unreachable button, can somehow be maneuvered into 275 horribly uncomfortable positions. The way you look at yourself. The way your kids look at you.

A week earlier, I had promised my son that his mother and I wouldn't die for a "very, very long time"—and here I was, closer to death than any human being he'd ever seen.

The first thing he said upon seeing me strapped into a wheelchair and hauled off to who-knows-where was that I had lied to him. His mother defended me. But she couldn't convince the boy that I'd ever walk again. That's what wheelchairs mean to a child.

As it turned out, my legs were in fine shape. Intestinally, though, I was a mess. In just a few weeks I lost fifty pounds—which impressed some of my chubbier friends until 1) they got a good look at me in a well-lit room, 2) they learned that the tab for the Burkett Quick Weight-Loss Program hovers around $125,000, or 3) I'd mention that forty-five of those lost pounds had once been fairly important organs.

For that kind of money, you can have unimportant organs removed. Painlessly. At your convenience.

My two-year-old daughter loved to visit me in the hospital because they handed out free lollipops to kids in the gift shop. But my son wanted nothing to do with the place or, it seemed, me. The first few times he was dragged to my bedside, he couldn't look me in the eye or offer more than a monotone "Hi, Dad." He'd bring a canvas bag full of toys to help him pretend he was somewhere else. Anywhere else.

It was certainly understandable. I looked like I was gonna die. I *felt* like I was gonna die. Everyone *acted* like I was gonna die. How does a kid deal with something as incomprehensible as the impending loss of a parent? By doing whatever he can to keep from thinking about it, I discovered.

While my son wouldn't talk to me, he made fast friends with my roommate—a fellow named John, in his early fifties, who was battling an advanced case of pancreatic cancer.

John was in incredible pain, always, yet he somehow seemed more concerned with my recovery than his own. Perhaps for the same reason my son needed his toys for distraction.

The only time John talked of himself, he talked of the future. Of how he was going to quit smoking once and for all. Of how he was going to start spending less time working and more time with his family. Of how he was going to try harder to understand his three grown children.

Two days before I was to be sent home, John died. That evening, one of his daughters came to my room, stood by my bed, and silently held my hand, as if she couldn't find the words to console *me*. Where does such compassion come from? Her father, I thought.

During my son's next visit, he asked about John. The truth was followed by a long, stunned silence.

"For reals?" he said.

"Yes. For reals."

"But Dad ... you said people die when they get old. John wasn't old."

"No, he wasn't. But he was in a lot of pain. Now he doesn't hurt anymore."

We both cried.

It took a lot of courage for him to ask his next question.

"Dad, tell me the truth. Are you gonna die, too?"

"No, sweetheart. The doctors are going to make me better, and I'll come home, and everything will be just like it was. But until then, I'll need your help, okay? I'll need you to be brave and not to worry and to help your mother and sister around the house. Can you do that for me?"

"Yes." Pause. "If you promise not to die."

I promised. Because sometimes, lies and stretched truths and hopes and love and being a parent are the same thing.

"Dad," he said, picking up his bag of toys. "Would you like to play dinosaurs with me?"

Yes, son. More than ever.

Exit Lines

Maybe it was the Continuous-Feed Morphine Machine, the hoses up my nose, the broad assortment of IV tubes connected to my arms and neck, or the three-and-a-half weeks I spent with Norma the Night Nurse from Hell. But there were moments during my hospitalization when I thought, "Hmmm. Maybe I'm not gonna live forever, after all."

This was not a brand-new possibility. It had occurred to me twice before, both times in a delivery room. It's amazing; one minute you're immortal, the next you're holding a tiny, loud, wet, purple baby and feeling as vulnerable as the flame on a birthday candle. In the path of a Florida hurricane.

You become instantly desperate to see your child grow up. To see what kind of human being you've foisted on the world. To see what kind of world you've foisted on him. To be the first to rush the stage when he's named Athlete of the Year or Burger King Employee of the Month or Most-Improved Inmate of Cellblock Six.

So you worry: What if the brakes snap at 75 mph or the engines conk out at thirty thousand feet or a sniper gets me in his crosshairs or all my years of idiotic, self-destructive behavior catch up with me in some dark alley?

What if I miss it all?

Eventually, after about three nanoseconds, you realize it's just too damned hard to think about. But the question returns to haunt you every now and again—like when you're in the hospital, unable to move, with shaky vital signs and a bloodstream larded with emotion-magnifying painkillers that make you sob uncontrollably at the drop of a moderately sincere "Hi" from the guy who's come to empty your wastebasket.

What if I miss it all?

It was *still* too hard to think about. Somehow, this was easier: Let's say I will indeed die in the hands of Norma the Night Nurse from Hell, and have only two minutes to tell my kids everything I want them to know. What would I say?

Clichés, mostly. Gooey, goopy, sloppy, obvious, discount-greeting-card, morphine-enhanced, straight-from-the-soul clichés.

First off, I thought, I'd tell them that the hardest mistakes to learn from are the mistakes you make when you mistakenly thought you'd learned from your mistakes—and that if they ever presume this fact has at long last sunk into their skull pudding, they're almost certainly mistaken.

That one perfect diamond may be worth a quarter-ton of rhinestones, but the whole truckload isn't worth a single, badly connected phone call from an old friend you thought you'd lost.

That all searches for forgiveness are best begun in front of a mirror.

That pain is a handy reminder you're still alive—and that joy wouldn't be nearly so popular without it.

That the world is whatever you make of it, not what it makes of you.

That in all contests between the mind and heart, the smart money's on the more southerly organ—no matter how often it ends up breaking.

I'd tell them that when they can no longer think of a good, solid reason to laugh at themselves every two minutes or so, it's high time to loosen up.

That if they like black-velvet, Day-Glo Elvis paintings or pink flamingo lawn decorations, screw everyone and buy 'em by the crate.

That the easy way out of any situation always evolves into the hard way out. Sooner or later.

That some people will dislike them for dumb reasons, some people will dislike them for imaginary reasons, and some people will dislike them for no reason at all. Let them.

I'd point out that they beat incredible odds just to exist; unbelievable odds to exist *right now* in the flerzillion-year span of creation; and flat-out impossible odds to exist *right here,* surrounded as they are by ardent admirers with a serious kiss-hug fetish. Such luck, I would add, is not to be taken lightly.

Finally, I'd wish them the happiest lives in the history of mankind ...and suggest that, one day, they should have children of their own for some really terrific company.

My emotional slobbering concluded and my two minutes up, I will proceed to slip into The Great Beyond. And I know exactly what my kids will say.

"Huh?...Was he talking to US?...Dad? Were you talking to US?... Dad?...Dad?..."

ACKNOWLEDGMENTS

This part of a book is like the end credits of a movie; by now, most folks are out in the parking lot searching for their car keys. But for those who have remained seated, *The Dad Zone* has been brought to you by the help, guidance and inspiration of:

Jana Bommersbach, the best damned full-service friend in creation ... Deborah Block, Sarah Wallace, and Elizabeth Andersen, the best damned copyeditors in creation ... Lee Salem of Universal Press Syndicate, a fine pen pal ... my agent, Edward Dunbar, who deserves to be spared when they make it legal to kill lawyers ... and Mary Duffield, the Santa Cruz High School journalism teacher who gave me my first weekly newspaper column and never admitted out loud that it was a huge mistake.

Plus, thanks and love to David, Lisa and Archie, Sandy Wyman, Normann Pesenti, Joe Axton, Dewey Webb, Bill and Betty Kress, Bill Kress Jr., Mark and Nancy Messerly, Mary Helen McGinn, Kelly Maloney, Dan Harkins, Max McQueen, Jami McFerren, Diane Bonilla, Rosemary Scarfo, Caroline Szatkowski, Pat McMahon, John Beasley, John Kopaz, Dave Walker, Don Harris, Gayle Tanber, Naomi Morgan, Pat Broeske, Erin Quinn, Hosea and Carrie Graham ... and Susanne Jaffe, the best damned book editor in creation. Despite what Jana says.